Sew-licious

LITTLE THINGS

Sew-licious
LITTLE THINGS

35 ZAKKA SEWING PROJECTS TO MAKE LIFE MORE BEAUTIFUL

Kate Haxell

CICO BOOKS
LONDON NEW YORK

Published in 2015 by CICO Books
An imprint of Ryland Peters & Small Ltd
20–21 Jockey's Fields, London WC1R 4BW
341 E 116th St, New York, NY 10029
www.rylandpeters.com

10 9 8 7 6 5 4 3 2 1

A CIP catalog record for this book is
available from the Library of Congress
and the British Library.

ISBN: 978-1-78249-190-3

Printed in China

Editor: Katie Hardwicke
Designer: Elizabeth Healey
Photographer: Joanna Henderson
Illustrator: Carrie Hill
Technique and template artworks:
  Stephen Dew
Stylists: Sania Pell and Luis Peral

Editor: Carmel Edmonds
In-house designer: Fahema Khanam
Art director: Sally Powell
Head of production: Patricia Harrington
Publishing manager: Penny Craig
Publisher: Cindy Richards

**NOTE: All instructions in this book contain
both standard (imperial) and metric
measurements. Please use only one set
of measurements when cutting out and
sewing, as they are not interchangeable.**

Contents

"Creativity is contagious; pass it on." Albert Einstein

"It is the small things that make life good." Sebastian Vettel

Introduction

The physicist Albert Einstein and the Formula 1 racing driver Sebastian Vettel must be pretty low down on the list of People Most Likely To Appear In The Introduction To A Sewing Book, but here they both are in this one. It's not their sewing skills that are putting them here (tempting though it is to think of Seb sitting in the pits doing some needlepoint), it's things they've said—the words at the top of this page.

I'm not really one for inspirational quotes—the nugget of truth they contain is too often drowned in a sea of sentimentality—but sometimes a few words really do sum up something you want to say, and both of these quotes do just that.

I firmly believe that creativity is contagious, and that it's a solemn duty to pass it on. And with this book I'm doing my very best to spread the creativity virus far and wide. Whether you're a newbie sewist looking for something simple and sweet (maybe try Party Time, page 52, or Scentilicious, page 106), a keen knitter (Knitting Know-How, page 86, or Lovely Colors, page 90 should do it for you), a fan of hand stitching (Go Fish, page 76, or Keyed Up, page 54, might be your thing), a dog owner (Bone Fidos, page 123, or Puppy Purse, page 14 should keep you and your hound happy), a master machinist (have a look at Washed Up, page 18, or Bagged Up, page 34), a gadget geek (turn to Take Your Tablet, page 66, or Love Your Laptop, page 10) a devoted crafter, a keen cook, a dedicated shopper, a fan of exercise... There are perfectly practical projects for all sorts of interests, tastes, and skills in this book, so I hope that you do catch something creatively inspiring from me.

What all the projects have in common is that they are small, and they are practical, and while the Japanese zakka ethos has various attributes—depending on who you ask and which aspect of zakka you're looking at—when it comes to handmade zakka, those two characteristics are essential. Along with good looks...

Many of the projects in this book are small and simple, easy to achieve in an evening; others are equally small but will take a little more time. But either way—though I'm quite sure that Seb didn't have sewing on his mind when he made his pithy comment—small things do make life good, and there are 35 of them in this book, so that's a healthy dollop of goodness to sew. I hope you get as much pleasure from making them as I did.

May your bobbin always be full!

Kate

CHAPTER 1

FOR *carrying*

MY STUFF I NEED...

Love YOUR laptop,
AND KEEP IT SAFE

Make a padded-and-practical but good-looking bag to tote your laptop around in. I made my bag a patched one, but you can equally well use a single piece of fabric for the outside of the bag. The pattern is easy to adapt for any size of laptop; just measure carefully and work out the fabric quantities you need on paper before starting to cut.

YOU'RE GOING TO NEED...

- One piece of outer fabric and one piece of lining fabric: I joined several pieces of quilting cotton to make the outer fabric and used a single piece of cotton ticking for the lining—see Size Matters, below (and don't fret over the math, it's not tricky)
- One piece of wool batting (wadding) —size as above

- Strip of fabric and strip of medium-weight fusible interfacing each measuring 4in (10cm) x as-long-as-you-want-it plus ³/₄in (2cm) for the handle: my handle is 39in (100cm) long
- Two strips of bias-cut fabric measuring 1¹/₄in (3cm) x long-enough-to-loop-around-your-button plus 1¹/₄in (3cm) for the button loops— see Loop-the-Loop, on page 12

- Tape measure
- Fabric scissors
- Iron and ironing board
- Pins
- Sewing threads to match fabrics
- Sewing machine
- Hand-sewing needle

SIZE MATTERS

- Measure the width, length, and depth of your laptop.
- Cut one piece of outer fabric and one piece of lining fabric each measuring the width plus twice the depth plus 2in (5cm), by the length multiplied by 2.5 plus 1¹/₄in (3cm).
- Cut one piece of batting (wadding) that measures the width plus twice the depth plus 2in (5cm), by the length multiplied by 2 plus 1¹/₄in (3cm).

- Note that I have added 2in (5cm) to the width so that it's easy to get my laptop in and out of the bag: if you want a snugger fit, then add 1¹/₂in (4cm), but no less than that.
- For example, my laptop measures 12in (30cm) wide, by 8in (20cm) long, by ³/₈in (1cm) deep.
- So my pieces of outer fabric (the total size of the patched-together piece: see Step 3 for patch-piece sizes) and lining fabric are: 14³/₄ x 21¹/₄in (37 x 53cm).

Width: 12in (30cm) + ³/₈in (1cm) + ³/₈in (1cm) + 2in (5cm) = 14³/₄in (37cm)

Length: 8in (20cm) x 2.5 + 1¹/₄in (3cm) = 21¹/₄in (53cm)

- And my piece of batting is:

Width: 12in (30cm) + ³/₈in (1cm) + ³/₈in (1cm) + 2in (5cm) = 14³/₄in (37cm)

Length: 8in (20cm) x 2 + 1¹/₄in (3cm) = 17¹/₄in (43cm)

1 Matching three raw edges (both sides and the edge that will be the top edge of the front of the bag), lay the piece of batting on the wrong side of the lining. The strip of lining not covered by the batting will be the front flap. Treat these two pieces as one layer from now on.

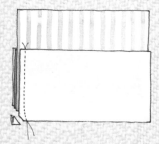

2 Right side in, fold the front edge of the lining up by the length of the laptop plus ⅝in (1.5cm) (in this case that's 8⅝in/21.5cm), so that the side edges and the top and bottom edges of the batting align. Taking a ⅝-in (1.5-cm) seam allowance, sew the side seams. Trim off the folded corners of the seam allowances at an angle. Leave this piece wrong side out.

3 To make my patched outer fabric, I sewed together three pieces measuring the width by 6¾in (17cm) and one piece measuring the width by 4¾in (11cm): this short piece is on the leading edge of the bag flap. These measurements include ⅝in (1.5cm) seam allowances, and I pressed the seam allowances open.

Fold the outer piece in the same way, then sew and clip the side seams as for the lining. Turn the outer right side out and press the seam allowances toward the front of the bag.

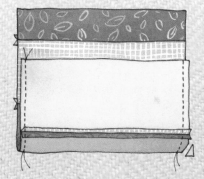

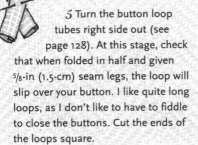

4 Right side in, fold each button loop strip in half lengthwise. Taking a ¹/₄-in (5-mm) seam allowance, sew along the long edge.

LOOP-THE-LOOP

For each button loop you need a strip of fabric that, when folded in half, will slip over your button, plus 1¹/₄in (3cm). The strip should be 1¹/₄in (3cm) wide and cut on the bias; that is, cut at a 45-degree angle across the fabric so that it is stretchy.

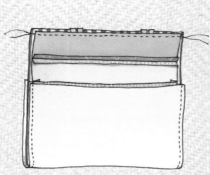

5 Turn the button loop tubes right side out (see page 128). At this stage, check that when folded in half and given ⁵/₈-in (1.5-cm) seam legs, the loop will slip over your button. I like quite long loops, as I don't like to have to fiddle to close the buttons. Cut the ends of the loops square.

6 On the outer bag, baste (tack) the loops to the right side of the edge of the front flap, matching the raw ends of the loop to the raw edge of the fabric. Lay the legs of the loop next to one another, as shown, to reduce bulk. I positioned the loops 4³/₄in (12cm) in from the edges of the bag flap; you can vary that, but they must be at least 4in (10cm) from the edges.

7 Slip the right-side-out outer bag into the inside-out lining, so that the right sides of the two fabrics are together. Pin the layers along the top edge of the flap, making sure that the button loops are lying flat and straight. Taking a ⁵/₈-in (1.5-cm) seam allowance, sew the seam.

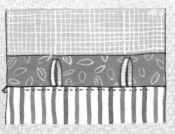

8 Pull the inner and outer bags apart again and lay the joined ends of the flap flat. Press the seam allowances toward the lining. Starting and stopping 2in (5cm) from the edges of the fabric, understitch the seam allowances to the lining to help prevent the lining from rolling forward and showing on the right side.

9 Slip the inner bag back into the outer and, making sure that the side seams match and that all layers are lying flat and unpuckered, pin the layers together around the raw edges of the flap and the top front edge of the bag. I like to baste this stage: it only takes five minutes and helps make sure everything is perfectly neat. Leave a 4-in (10-cm) gap in the middle of the front edge for turning through.

10 Starting from one side of this gap and taking a ⅝-in (1.5-cm) seam allowance, sew along the front edge to the side seam, then continue sewing 1¼in (3cm) past the seam onto the flap, making sure the seam allowances stay facing toward the front of the bag. With the needle down in the fabric, pivot and sew up to the top edge of the flap. Trim the flap seam allowance down to ⅝in (1.5cm) and clip into the corner you pivoted on, as shown. Trim off the corners of the seam allowances on the leading edge of the flap.

11 Turn the bag right side out through the gap, pulling both the lining and outer right side out. Push out the corners neatly. Then tuck the lining into the outer. Ease and press the seams, making sure the clipped corners are neat and flat. Ladder stitch (see page 131) the gap closed.

12 Iron the fusible interfacing onto the back of the handle fabric strip. Press under a ⅜-in (1-cm) hem at each short end of the handle. Right side in, fold the handle strip in half lengthwise. Taking a ⅝-in (1.5-cm) seam allowance, sew the long seam.

13 Turn the handle right side out and, with the seam along one edge, press it flat. Topstitch along both long edges, stitching ¼in (5mm) in from the edge. Baste the ends of the handle to the sides of the bag, centering each end over a side seam, 1½in (4cm) down from the front edge of the bag. (Make sure the handle isn't twisted before basting the second end in place.) Baste in a square at the bottom of the handle, as shown.

14 Now sew the handle in place, sewing in a square as for the basting, and sewing over the lines of topstitching done in Step 13. I reinforced the stitching by sewing a very tight zigzag around the square over the previous stitching. Remove the basting. Sew on buttons to align with the button loops.

Puppy PURSE

Have a pup to guard your pennies with this cute change purse. It's entirely hand stitched, but just with simple irregular blanket stitch, which is forgiving if you're an embroidery newbie. All zippers will be too long, but don't worry about that either, as they are very easy to shorten.

YOU'RE GOING TO NEED...

- Templates on page 132
- Two pieces of felt and two pieces of heavyweight fusible interfacing measuring 6in (15cm) square
- One piece of felt measuring $3\frac{1}{2} \times 2\frac{3}{4}$in (9 x 7cm): I used a piece of felted blanket
- Stranded embroidery flosses (threads): I used two shades of gray
- Button(s) for an eye: I used a black button topped by a tiny pearl one
- Small pom-pom for nose: I used one cut from pom-pom trimming
- Nylon-toothed zipper
- Paper for templates
- Paper scissors and fabric scissors
- Iron and ironing board
- Embroidery needle
- Pins
- Hand-sewing needle
- Sewing threads to sew on eye and to match zipper tape

1 Trace the templates on page 132 and cut out. Iron the fusible interfacing onto the backs of the large pieces of felt and cut out two puppy heads, remembering to flip the template before cutting the second head to produce a front and a back. Cut one ear from the small piece of felt.

2 Using three strands of embroidery floss (thread), and starting just behind the top curve of the ear, work irregular blanket stitch (see page 130) around the edge, fanning the stitches around the curves, finishing just in front of the top curve, as shown, but don't fasten off.

3 Pin the ear to the head that faces to the right, as positioned on the template. Continue the blanket stitching, but stitching the ear to the head rather than just edging the ear. Finish the stitching by taking the needle right through to the back of the head and fastening off.

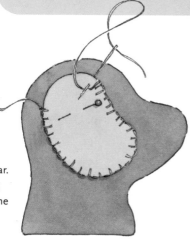

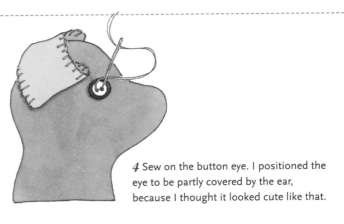

4 Sew on the button eye. I positioned the eye to be partly covered by the ear, because I thought it looked cute like that.

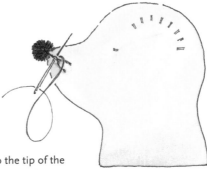

5 Sew the pom-pom to the tip of the snout. I used a pom-pom cut from trimming, so it had tails that I could sew to the interfacing on the back of the head. If you are using a pom-pom without tails, it will be easier to sew it on once the front and back of the purse are sewn together.

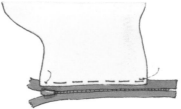

6 Starting at the open end of the zipper, baste (tack) the tape to the straight edge across the bottom of the dog's neck. Position the zipper so that—when it's closed—the pull is just a tiny way back from the front edge of the neck, and about two-thirds of the tape is overlapping the neck.

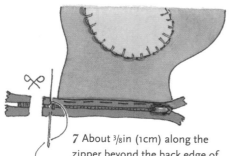

7 About ³⁄₈in (1cm) along the zipper beyond the back edge of the neck, whip stitch (see page 129) over the teeth, then cut off any excess zipper just beyond the stitching: don't use your fabric scissors for this as it will blunt the blades.

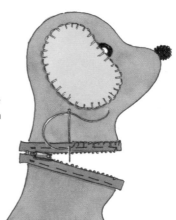

8 Pin the heads wrong sides together at the base of the neck. Fold the free zipper tape up over the back head so that the zipper teeth run exactly along the base of the necks, then baste the tape to the back head only. Unpin the heads.

9 Open the zipper. At the pull end, fold the tape over the edge of the neck, making sure the fold is square, then blanket stitch the edge of the tape to the neck. Use doubled sewing thread that matches the zipper tape and make the stitches irregular, as before.

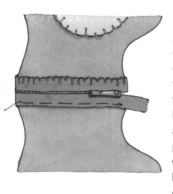

10 Before you get to the other end of the tape, close the zipper, then fold the cut end over to the back of the neck, keeping the fold square, and blanket stitch it in place. Fasten off on the wrong side. Remove the basting stitches. Blanket stitch the other edge of the tape to the back head in the same way. Iron patches of fusible interfacing over visible stitching on the back of the head, just to protect it from coins when the purse is used.

11 Pin the heads together. Using matching sewing thread, whip stitch the folded ends of the zipper tapes together. Then use three strands of embroidery floss and irregular blanket stitch to sew the heads together all around the edges. Open the zipper to fasten off the thread on the inside of the purse.

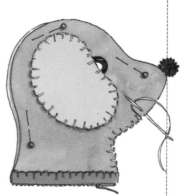

Washed UP

• •

I made this as a weekend washbag; it's perfect for the travel-sized lotions and potions I take with me when I'm only away for a couple of days. Choose cotton fabrics so that the bag is washable if anything leaks.

YOU'RE GOING TO NEED...

- Templates on page 136
- One piece of fabric measuring 12 x 8in (30 x 20cm), one piece measuring 13 x 6in (33 x 15cm), and one piece measuring 9 x 3in (23 x 8cm): I used quilting cottons
- 8-in (20-cm) zipper
- Paper for templates
- Paper scissors and fabric scissors
- Tape measure
- Iron and ironing board
- Pins
- Sewing threads to match fabrics
- Sewing machine with zipper foot
- Hand-sewing needle

1 Enlarge the templates on page 136 by 200 percent. Cut out one back from the largest piece of fabric, one bottom front from the middle-sized piece, and one top front from the smallest piece.

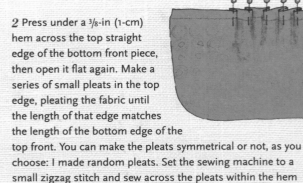

2 Press under a 3/8-in (1-cm) hem across the top straight edge of the bottom front piece, then open it flat again. Make a series of small pleats in the top edge, pleating the fabric until the length of that edge matches the length of the bottom edge of the top front. You can make the pleats symmetrical or not, as you choose: I made random pleats. Set the sewing machine to a small zigzag stitch and sew across the pleats within the hem to hold them in place.

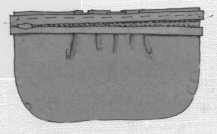

3 Position one of the zipper tapes right side down on the right side of the pleated hem, so that the endstop is 5/8in (1.5cm) from the edge and the pressed edge of the hem is against the zipper teeth. Baste (tack) the tape in place. Using a zipper foot, sew the tape in place, sewing very close to the teeth.

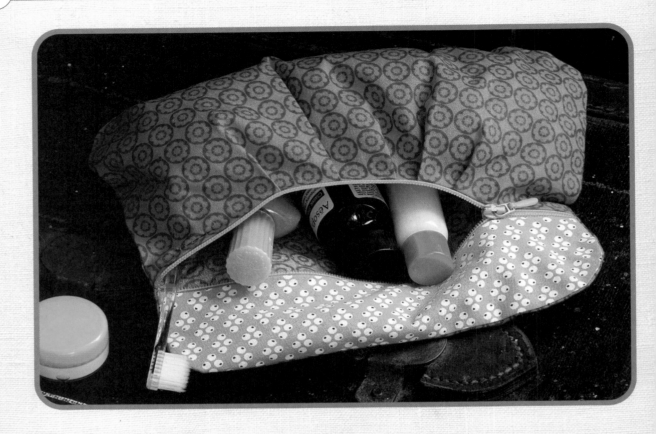

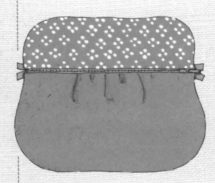

4 In the same way as in Step 3, and taking a ³/₈-in (1-cm) seam allowance, baste and then sew the other zipper tape to the bottom edge of the top front. Neaten the seam allowances by trimming them to the width of the tapes and then zigzagging the tape to the fabric.

5 Oversew the ends of the zipper tapes together. Undo the zipper halfway.

6 Pin the front and back right sides together, matching the raw edges and easing the pieces to fit as needed. Taking a ³/₈-in (1-cm) seam allowance, sew all around the edges. Zigzag and trim the seam allowances, then turn the bag right side out through the zipper. Press the seams flat.

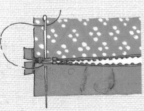

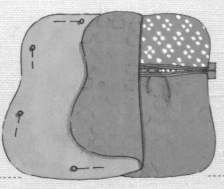

Pinned OUT

A laundry-day staple, the humble clothespin bag can be a thing of beauty without losing an ounce of practicality. And you can make it whatever size you want. Big family? Make a big bag for maximum clothespin storage. I made my clothespin bag from patched-together scraps, but you can make yours from whatever fabrics you like best.

YOU'RE GOING TO NEED...

- Wooden coat hanger
- Fabric, or fabrics, large enough to make up your paper pattern: see Steps 1 and 2
- Two pieces of bias binding the width of the clothespin bag
- Saw, if you want your bag to be smaller than the full width of the hanger: I sawed 1½in (4cm) off each end of my hanger
- Paper for templates
- Paper scissors and fabric scissors
- Ruler and pencil
- Tape measure
- Iron and ironing board
- Pins
- Sewing threads to match fabrics
- Sewing machine

1 Draw a paper pattern for your clothespin bag. Lay the hanger on a piece of paper and draw around the top edge, marking the position of the hook. Using a ruler, draw a line from the tip of one end of the hanger straight across to the tip of the other end. Then draw a line below that one at the depth you want the bag to be: mine is 9in (23cm) deep. Draw straight lines down from the tips of the hanger to the bottom edge line, and that is the basic pattern for the overall shape of the bag. You can alter the template shape a bit if you wish: I re-drew the vertical lines to flare out slightly, then curved the bottom corners.

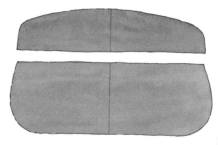

2 To ensure that your pattern is symmetrical, fold it in half at the mid-point (where the hook emerges), then cut it out through both layers. This piece is the back template. Cut out a second identical paper pattern for the front, but cut that in two across the width, 3½in (9cm) down from the top of the hanger. You need to add ⅝in (1.5cm) for seam allowances and ease around all edges, so either do this on the paper before you cut out the patterns, or add it when you cut out the fabric.

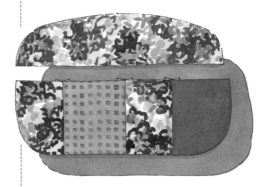

3 You can cut all the pieces from one fabric, or you can do as I did, and use several fabrics. I cut the back from teal linen and the front top from needlecord, and I patched together four pieces of three different fabrics to make the front bottom.

6 On the right side, sewing ¼in (5mm) in from the edge, topstitch right across the hemmed edge of the front top and bottom pieces.

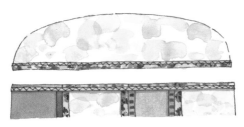

4 On the right side, fold and pin a length of bias binding over the raw straight edge of the front top and bottom pieces of the clothespin bag. Set the sewing machine to a narrow zigzag and sew the binding in place. Press the bound edges under to the wrong side by ⅜in (1cm) to make a hem.

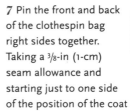

5 Unfold the pressed hems and, right sides together, pin the front top and bottom pieces together along the pressed lines. Sewing from each end toward the middle, sew along 3¼in (8cm) of the seam, sewing along the pressed lines, leaving an opening in the middle.

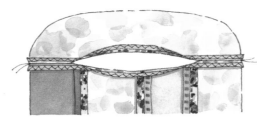

7 Pin the front and back of the clothespin bag right sides together. Taking a ⅜-in (1-cm) seam allowance and starting just to one side of the position of the coat hanger hook (mark this with a vertical pin), sew around the edges, stopping and reversing just before the starting point to leave a gap for the hook.

8 Zigzag and trim the seam allowances (remember not to zigzag over the gap for the hook), and turn the bag right side out. Insert the coat hanger through the opening, sliding the hook through the gap in the top.

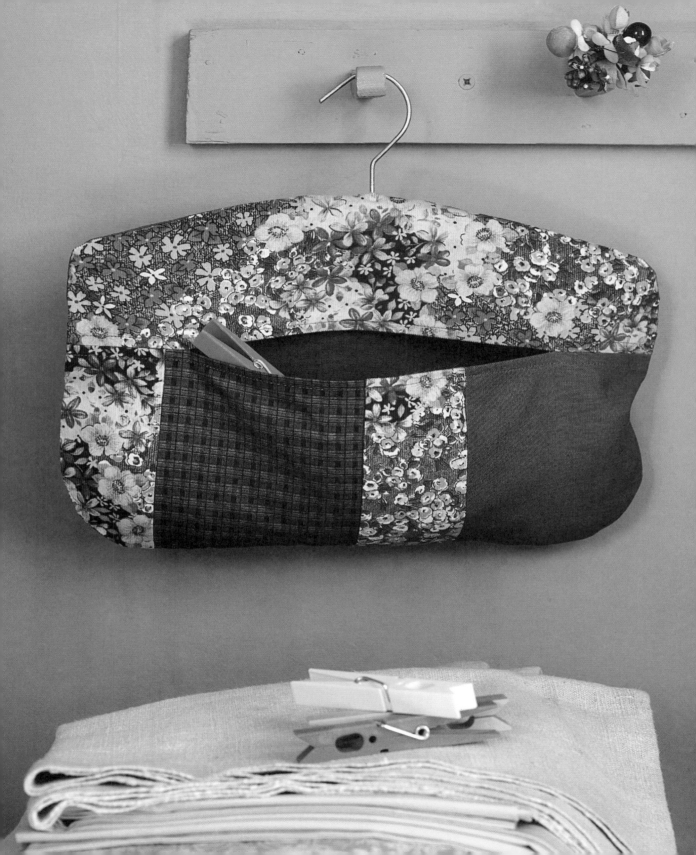

Totally PERFECT

Strong, secure, and seriously stylish, this is the perfect tote bag. The drawstring top pulls tight over your shopping to keep everything safe. For a quick-and-easy tote, you can simply leave out the lining and drawstring sections and just hem the top edge of the bag.

YOU'RE GOING TO NEED...

- Fabric and cord: see How Much Fabric?, right
- Tassel or charm, if required
- Tape measure
- Fabric scissors
- Iron and ironing board
- Pins
- Pinking shears
- Sewing threads to match fabrics
- Sewing machine
- Fading fabric marker
- Hand-sewing needle

HOW MUCH FABRIC?

You can make a tote bag almost any size you want. You'll need:

- Two pieces of medium- to heavyweight outer fabric measuring the width of the bag plus 1¼in (3cm), by the length of the bag plus 1¼in (3cm)
- Two pieces of light- to medium-weight lining fabric measuring the width of the bag plus 1¼in (3cm), by the length of the bag plus 1¼in (3cm)
- Two pieces of light- to medium-weight fabric for the drawstring top measuring the width of the bag plus 1¼in (3cm), by one-third of the length of the bag plus 2in (5cm)
- Two pieces of medium- to heavyweight handle fabric measuring twice the finished width plus 1¼in (3cm), by the length plus 1¼in (3cm)
- Two lengths of ribbon or cord twice the width of the bag plus 6in (15cm): I used suede ribbon

1 Right sides together and taking a ⅝-in (1.5-cm) seam allowance, sew the two outer pieces together around three sides, leaving the short top edge open. Sew the lining in the same way, but leave a 4-in (10-cm) gap in the middle of the short bottom edge. At the top open edge, press about 1in (2.5cm) of the seams open. Turn the outer piece right side out, but leave the lining wrong side out.

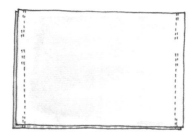

2 Pin the drawstring pieces right sides together. Starting at the top edge and taking a ⁵⁄₈-in (1.5-cm) seam allowance, sew 1³⁄₈in (3.5cm) of one side seam, then reverse to secure the stitches. Leave a ³⁄₈-in (1-cm) gap, then sew the rest of the seam, reversing at each end. Sew the other side seam in the same way, then press both seams open and trim the seam allowances with pinking shears.

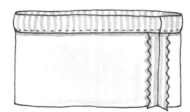

3 Press under a ³⁄₈-in (1-cm) then a ³⁄₄-in (2-cm) hem around the top edge of the drawstring piece. Sew the hem very close to the bottom edge to make a channel for the drawstring. The gaps in the side seam should now be in the middle of the hem on the right side of the piece.

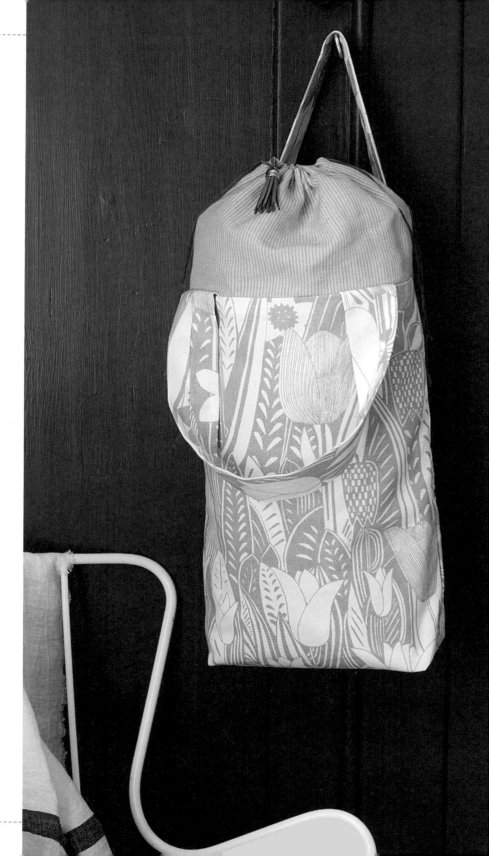

4 Right side in, fold a handle strip in half lengthwise. Taking a ⅝-in (1.5-cm) seam allowance, sew the seam. Press the seam open, then turn the handle right side out (see page 128). Roll the seam to the center back and press the handle flat. Repeat for the other handle strip.

5 Seam uppermost, pin and then zigzag stitch a handle to the top edge of the right side of the front and back of the bag. Make sure that the handles aren't twisted before you sew them on.

6 Right sides together, slip the drawstring section over the top of the outer bag, matching the side seams and the raw bottom edge of the drawstring section with the raw top edge of the bag.

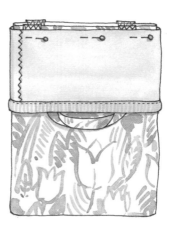

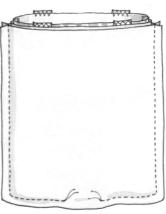

7 Next, slip the outer bag/drawstring pieces into the inside-out lining, matching the side seams and the raw top edge of the lining with the already matched raw edges of the outer and drawstring pieces. Pin all the layers together around the matched raw edges, then, taking a ⅝-in (1.5-cm) seam allowance, sew right around the top edge.

8 Pull the outer bag up out of the lining, and, with both layers inside out, make the square corners. Fold an outer-bag corner flat, so that the bottom seam aligns with a side seam, and pin the seams together through all the layers. Measure down the seam 2in (5cm) from the point, and draw a line across the corner, at right angles to the seam, as shown. Machine-sew along this line, reversing at both ends to secure the stitching. Sew the other corner the same way, making sure that the seam allowance is lying to the same side.

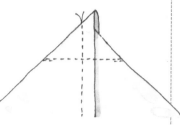

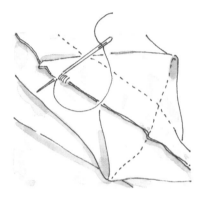

9 At the sewn line, fold each corner over toward the bottom of the bag and hand sew the point to the seam allowance of the bottom seam. Repeat Steps 8 and 9 on the corners of the lining.

10 Turn the whole bag out through the gap in the lining, pulling the outer bag through, then continuing to pull until the lining is right side out, too. Press under the seam allowances across the gap in the lining, then sew the gap closed; either machine-sew very close to the edge, as I have, or use ladder stitch (see page 131). Tuck the lining down inside the bag and press the seam around the top edge flat.

11 Thread the ribbon through one side of the channel in the drawstring section, from one gap in the side seam to the other gap. Thread on a tassel or charm, if you want, then thread the ribbon through the other side of the channel to come out through the first gap again. Knot the ends of the ribbon together. Repeat the process with the second length of ribbon, but starting at the opposite gap to the first ribbon.

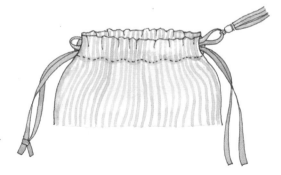

Patched UP

Drawstring bags are easy to make in any size your heart desires, and have a zillion uses: weekend-away laundry, special shoe storage, superlative gift wrap, craft project storage, bridesmaids' bags, knitting carry-all, vacation washbag, sports kit... For non-utility bags, make patched versions that are great stash busters, as well as looking lovely.

YOU'RE GOING TO NEED...

- Fabric, lace, and cord: see How Much Fabric?, below
- Tape measure
- Fabric scissors
- Iron and ironing board
- Pins
- Sewing threads to match fabrics
- Sewing machine
- Hand-sewing needle
- Small plate
- Fabric marker

HOW MUCH FABRIC?

To make a bag measuring 10⅝ x 15⅛in (27 x 38.5cm) from three fabrics, you'll need:

- One piece of fabric measuring 6¾ x 23in (17 x 58cm), one piece measuring 4¾ x 23in (12 x 58cm), and one piece measuring 8¾ x 23in (22 x 58cm)
- Piece of lace measuring 23in (58cm) long
- Two pieces of narrow ribbon or thin cord, each measuring 35in (90cm) long

1 Baste the lace to the top edge of the piece of fabric that will be at the bottom of the bag. Position it so that when the piece of fabric is sewn to the next piece taking a ⅜-in (1-cm) seam allowance, the top edge of the lace will be caught in the seam: the exact position of the lace depends on what the top edge looks like.

2 Right sides together, pin the middle piece to the bottom piece. Taking a ⅜-in (1-cm) seam allowance, sew the seam, catching the edge of the lace. Zigzag or serge (overlock) the seam allowances together. Press the seam flat, pressing the seam allowances upward.

3 Along the top edge of the top piece, press under a ⅜-in (1-cm) and then a 2-in (5-cm) hem. Sew the other long edge to the raw edge of the middle piece.

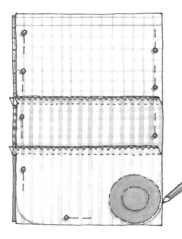

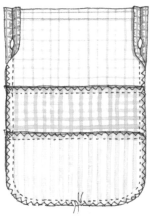

4 Fold the whole piece in half lengthwise, at right angles to the seams, and press the fold, then cut it in two along the fold to make two identical pieces. Open out the pressed hems along the top and pin the two pieces right sides together, matching the seams carefully. Use a plate and fabric marker to round off the bottom corners.

5 Sew from the middle of the bottom edge to 4¼in (10.5cm) from the top, then reverse to secure the stitches. Leave a ⅜-in (1-cm) gap and then sew the rest of the side seam to the top. Repeat the process to sew the other side seam from the middle of the bottom edge up to the top. From the top downward, press the seam allowances open to just below the gap. Zigzag the rest of the seam allowances and trim them.

6 Re-fold the pressed top hems. Sew around close to the lower edge, then sew a second line ¾in (2cm) above the first to make a channel: the gaps in the side seams should be within the channel. Turn right side out.

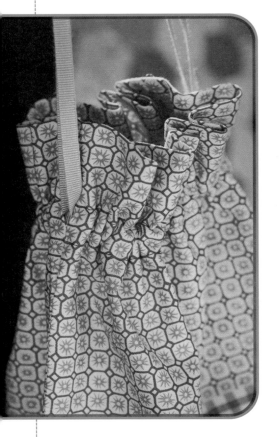

7 Thread one length of ribbon through one gap and right around the channel to come out of the same gap. Knot the ends together. Repeat the process with the second ribbon, taking it in and out of the other gap and then knotting the ends. Pull the strings to close the bag.

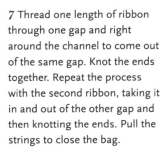

Pocket POUCH

Shopping baskets and totes are a good-looking and green alternative to plastic carriers, but everything small does end up in a jumble in the bottom, which is a pain when your phone rings or you need to find a pen. So, solve the problem with a detachable pocket that loops around the handles of your basket and hangs down safely inside it. You can adjust the size of your pocket to suit your bag, and make the pocket divisions to suit your stuff.

YOU'RE GOING TO NEED...

- Fabric and ribbon: see How Much Fabric?, below
- Two buttons with shanks
- Tape measure
- Fabric scissors
- Iron and ironing board
- Pins
- Sewing threads to match fabrics
- Sewing machine
- Hand-sewing needle

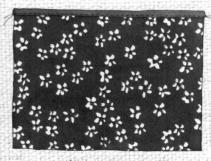

1 Press the 9⁵⁄₈in (24.5cm) length of ribbon in half lengthwise. Pin it across the top edge of the front pocket piece, encasing the raw edge. Sew it in place, sewing close to the open edge.

HOW MUCH FABRIC?

For a pocket that measures 8⁷⁄₈ x 9¹⁄₂in (22.5 x 24cm) and hangs 2in (5cm) down inside a bag that has handles 6¹⁄₄in (16cm) apart, you'll need:

- Piece of medium-weight fabric measuring 9⁵⁄₈ x 10¹⁄₄in (24.5 x 26cm) for pocket back and piece measuring 9⁵⁄₈ x 7¹⁄₄in (24.5 x 18.5cm) for pocket front
- Piece of heavyweight fabric measuring 9⁵⁄₈ x 10¹⁄₄in (24.5 x 26cm) for pocket backing
- Piece of heavyweight fusible interfacing measuring 8⁷⁄₈ x 9¹⁄₂in (22.5 x 24cm)
- One length of ⁵⁄₈-in (1.5-cm) ribbon, 9⁵⁄₈ (24.5cm) long, and two lengths 14¹⁄₂in (37cm) long

2 Right side up, lay the front piece on the right side of the back piece, matching the bottom and side raw edges. Baste (tack) the layers together.

3 Fold both of the 14½in (36cm) lengths of ribbon in half widthwise, making sure the loops are not twisted. Pin and then baste the raw ends of one loop to the top edge of the pocket, positioning it 1½in (4cm) in from the edge. Baste the other loop to the opposite edge of the pocket, positioning it the same distance from that edge. Pin the loops to the middle of the pocket to keep them square to the edge and out of the way of the stitching.

4 Round off all the corners of the fusible interfacing: you can use a coin to draw a curve if you want. Iron the fusible interfacing onto the wrong side of the backing piece of fabric, centering it carefully. Lay the backing piece right side down on top of the front piece, matching all edges.

5 Taking a ⅜-in (1-cm) seam allowance and leaving a 3¼-in (8-cm) gap in one side edge, sew the layers together around the edges, sewing just outside the edge of the fusible interfacing. Trim the seam allowances to ¼in (5mm), other than over the gap in the stitching. Remove the basting stitches.

6 Turn the pocket right side out through the gap. Press the pocket flat, then ladder stitch the gap closed (see page 131). If you wish, you can sew lines to divide the pocket into smaller sections: I've sewn one line, 3½in (9cm) from one edge. Start sewing the division from the base of the pocket. Reverse to secure the stitching, then use a sewing needle to take the ends of thread into the inside of the pocket.

7 Sew on buttons at the base of each loop. To attach the pocket to the bag, pass the loops around the handles and slip them over the buttons.

- Fabric for the outer and the lining:
  see How Much Fabric?, below
- Five buttons: I used five different
  vintage ones
- Tape measure
- Fabric scissors
- Iron and ironing board
- Pins
- Sewing threads to match fabrics
- Sewing machine
- Fabric marker
- Hand-sewing needle

HOW MUCH FABRIC?

- This bag measures 10¼ x 8¼in
  (26 x 21cm). For this you need:
- Three strips of fabric for straps:
  mine all measured 3 x 7in
  (8 x 18cm).
- One piece of outer fabric and
  one piece of lining fabric each
  measuring 11 x 23in (28 x 59cm).
  I made my outer fabric from two
  pieces sewn together, one 11 x 8in
  (28 x 22cm) piece for the front
  panel (the plain brown needlecord)
  and one 11 x 15½in (28 x 39cm)
  piece for the back and flap
  (measurements include extra
  seam allowances for joining the
  two pieces). I used needlecord
  for the outer fabric and cotton for
  the lining.

Bagged UP

This neat little bag offers some extra carrying space on your bike and, when detached, works as a hand-carry bag, too. You need to be able to make buttonholes, either by hand (if you are the patient type...) or on the sewing machine, and the size of the finished bag can be adapted to fit your own bike.

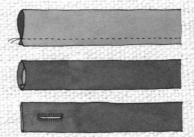

1 Right side in, fold each strap strip in half lengthwise. Taking a ⅜-in (1-cm) seam allowance, sew the long edge. Turn the tube right side out (see page 128). With the seam along one edge, press the tube flat. Turn in and press ⅜in (1cm) at each end of each strap. Make a buttonhole on one end of each of the three straps, through both layers.

2 Fold one strap 2½in (6cm) from the end without the buttonhole and lay it buttonhole-side up on the back of the outer bag, matching the fold with the raw side edge. The precise position of this strap depends on your bike; this is the strap that goes around the saddle bar. Baste (tack) across the folded end and along the length of the strap to keep it square to the edge of the fabric.

3 Fold the front section of the outer fabric up over the strap. If your bag is one piece of fabric, then fold up 8¼in (21cm) to make the front panel. Taking a ⅜-in (1-cm) seam allowance, sew down each side of the outer bag, reversing at the ends to secure the stitches. Clip off the bottom corners of the seam allowances.

4 Turn the outer right side out and fold the seam allowances forward toward the front of the bag. On the wrong side of the back, measure in ⅜in (1cm) from the side seam and make a mark. Repeat on the other side.

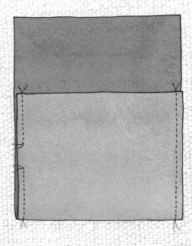

5 Fold and sew the lining in the same way as the outer bag, leaving a gap about 3in (8cm) long in the middle of one side seam. Leave the lining inside out.

6 Slip the outer bag inside the lining, so the right sides are together, matching the raw edges. Pin the layers together around the raw edges. At this stage you can, if you wish (and I did), shape the front edge of the flap. Draw the shape on the wrong side of the outer bag.

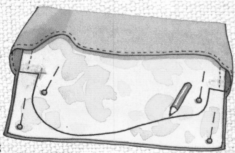

7 Taking a ³/₈-in (1-cm) seam allowance, sew right around the raw edges. Start on one side of the front edge, sew across it, sewing past the side seam to the mark made in Step 4. Pivot at this mark and sew around the front edge of the flap, then down the side of the flap to the mark adjacent to the other side seam. Pivot again, then finish sewing across the front edge.

8 Trim the seam allowances around the curves and cut notches in them (see page 128). Clip into the corner you pivoted on, as shown.

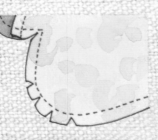

9 Turn the bag right side out through the gap in the lining, pulling the outer bag through, then continuing to pull until the whole thing is right side out. Press all the seams flat. Ladder stitch (see page 131) the gap closed. Topstitch around the open edges of the bag and flap, sewing 1/8in (2–3mm) in from the edge.

10 Make two buttonholes in the front flap. They can be positioned as you wish to suit the shape of your flap and your buttons.

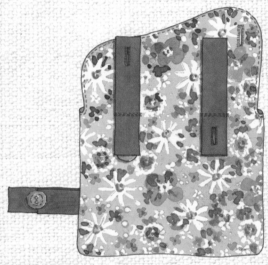

11 Fold the front flap over and press it lightly to mark the top edge. Open the flap out and lay the bag flat, front down. Lay the handle strips right side down on the bag, with the buttonhole end of one strap and the plain end of the other toward the front flap. Position the straps so that 4³⁄₈in (11cm) of each protrudes beyond the pressed line. The straps can be as widely spaced as suits your bag: these straps are 1½in (4cm) in from each edge. Sew across each strap on the pressed line, sewing back and forth a couple of times for strength.

12 Sew on buttons to match the buttonholes: one button on the end of each strap, and two on the front of the bag.

Tied UP

These soft bags can be made to whatever size suits you: a small one to stash in your purse for emergency shopping; a medium one to take books, sunscreen, and a wrap to the beach on vacation; a large one to go shopping in the market... The bag is reversible, but I've called the fabrics inner and outer for the sake of clarity.

1 Enlarge the template on page 140 by 400 percent. Fold a piece of fabric in half lengthwise and pin the template to it with the short straight edge against the fold. Cut out the piece and unfold it to produce one full-size outer piece. Cut out one more outer piece and two linings.

2 Pin the two outer pieces right sides together, matching the raw edges. Taking a ³/₈-in (1-cm) seam allowance, sew from the top of one handle down the long straight edge, across the bottom of the bag, then up the straight edge of the other handle to the top. Clip off the corners at the bottom, then press the seam allowances open. Repeat the process with the two inner pieces, but leave a 3-in (8-cm) gap in the middle of the bottom edge.

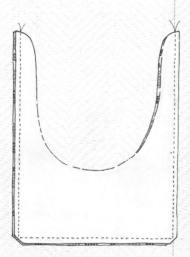

YOU'RE GOING TO NEED...

- Template on page 140
- Two pieces of outer fabric and two pieces of inner fabric each measuring 20 x 23¹/₂in (50 x 60cm): see How Much Fabric?, right
- Paper for template
- Paper scissors and fabric scissors
- Iron and ironing board
- Pins
- Sewing threads to match fabrics
- Sewing machine

HOW MUCH FABRIC?

- The long handles make the bag relatively fabric hungry, but one this size can be cut from two 25¹/₂-in (65-cm) lengths of 45-in (115-cm) wide fabric. Fold the fabric just wide enough to pin the template to the fold to cut out the first piece, then re-fold the fabric and pin the template to the other end, staggering the position of the handle relative to the first piece. Does that sound confusing? Try it (without cutting out) on a piece of fabric and it should make sense.

3 With the inner and outer bags both still inside out, make the square corners. Fold an outer-bag corner flat, so that the bottom seam aligns with a side seam, and pin the seams together through all the layers. Measure down the seam 2in (5cm) from the point, and draw a line across the corner, at right angles to the seam, as shown. Machine sew along this line, reversing at both ends to secure the stitching. Sew the other corner the same way.

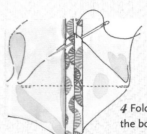

4 Fold each corner over toward the bottom of the bag at the sewn line and hand sew the point to the seam allowance of the bottom seam. Repeat Steps 3 and 4 on the corners of the inner bag.

5 Turn the outer bag right side out, but leave the inner bag inside out. Slip the outer bag into the inner, so that they are right sides together, matching the side seam and raw edges. Pin and then sew the pieces together all around the raw edges, taking a ³/₈-in (1-cm) seam allowance.

6 Clip notches (see page 128) in the seam allowances around the curved ends of the handles.

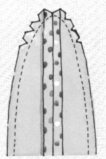

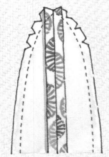

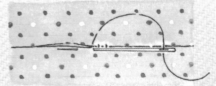

7 Turn the bag right side out through the gap in the inner, pushing out the handles carefully. Press the seams flat all round the edge of the bag. Ladder stitch (see page 131) the gap in the inner closed.

Card CARRYING

There are so many bits of plastic to carry around now: bank and credit cards, loyalty cards for everything from coffee to yarn, donor cards, travel card, business cards, car breakdown rescue card (it's a classic VW camper; breakdown cover isn't a luxury)... This neat little wallet will hold cards that aren't used very often and so don't need to be cluttering up your purse, plus you can stash a bit of emergency cash, just in case...

YOU'RE GOING TO NEED...

- One piece of fabric measuring $8^{1}/_{8}$ x $6^{1}/_{4}$in (20.5 x 16cm) and one piece of fusible webbing measuring $8^{1}/_{8}$ x $3^{1}/_{8}$in (20.5 x 8cm) for the first pocket
- One piece of fabric measuring $8^{1}/_{8}$ x 4in (20.5 x 10cm) and one piece of fusible webbing measuring $8^{1}/_{8}$ x 2in (20.5 x 5cm) for the second pocket
- Two pieces of fabric measuring $8^{1}/_{8}$ x $4^{3}/_{4}$in (20.5 x 12cm) and one piece of fusible webbing measuring $7^{3}/_{8}$ x 4in (18.5 x 10cm) for the cover
- 12in (30cm) of wide rick rack
- Snap fastener and decorative button
- Tape measure
- Fabric scissors
- Iron and ironing board
- Pins
- Sewing threads to match fabrics
- Sewing machine
- Hand-sewing needle

1 Right side out, press the two pocket pieces of fabric in half lengthwise. Slip the appropriate piece of fusible webbing between the layers and iron again to fuse them together.

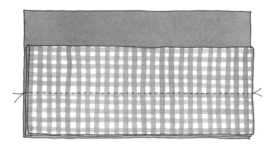

2 Iron the cover piece of fusible webbing onto the wrong side of the inner cover, centering it. Peel off the paper backing. Lay the inner cover right side up and pin the larger pocket on top of it, matching the bottom and side raw edges. Sew a line of stitching 1½in (4cm) up and parallel to the bottom edge, sewing through all layers.

3 Lay the smaller pocket on top of the first one, matching the raw edges as shown. Sew a vertical line up the middle, sewing through all layers and stopping at the top of the larger pocket. Leave long tails of thread. Use one thread tail and the hand-sewing needle to sew a few reinforcing stitches over the top edge of the pocket. Then take the tails through to the back and knot them securely.

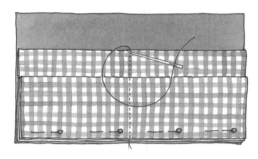

4 Turn under and sew a double hem on one end of the rick rack, folding it so that the scallops align. Sew one half of the snap fastener to the hem side, and sew the decorative button to the other side.

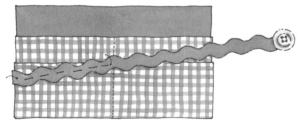

5 With the button facing up, baste (tack) the other end of the rick rack to the upper edge of the smaller pocket, positioning it as shown.

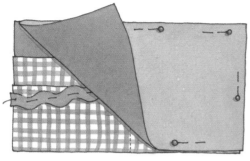

6 Fold and pin the rick rack to the pockets to keep it away from the edges. Then lay the remaining cover piece right side down on top. Pin the layers together: I basted them as well, just for accuracy.

7 Taking a ³⁄₈-in (1-cm) seam allowance, sew around the edges—following the line of the fusible webbing on the inner cover if that's easiest for you—leaving a gap in one side of the top edge. Carefully trim the seam allowances of the pocket pieces only, trimming them back to ¹⁄₈in (2–3mm).

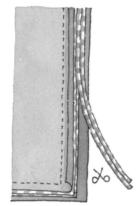

8 Turn the wallet right side out through the gap. Finger-press the seams very carefully, making sure they are perfectly aligned and that the seam allowances across the gap are turned in neatly, then press the cover with the iron, fusing the inner and outer cover together. Ladder stitch (see page 131) the gap closed.

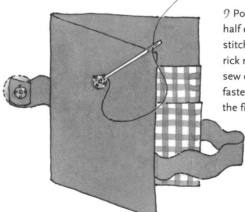

9 Pocket side in, fold the cover in half down the vertical line of stitching and press it. Wrap the rick rack around the wallet, then sew on the other half of the snap fastener to match the position the first half ends up in.

CHAPTER 2

TO KEEP *my stuff*

COZY I NEED...

Java JACKET

• • • • • • • • • • • • • • • •

I was always skeptical about the efficacy of java jackets; like a little scrap of fabric would make a difference to how long my coffee stayed hot... Then someone gave me one, and I was a convert. Plus it looked pretty, too. This version ties around your mug rather like an obi belt.

YOU'RE GOING TO NEED...

- One piece of lining fabric and one piece of wool batting (wadding), each measuring the height you want the jacket to be plus ³⁄₄in (2cm), by the circumference of the mug less the width of the handle and plus ³⁄₄in (2cm)
- Two pieces of fabric for the outer jacket that both measure the height you want the jacket to be: one piece should be two-thirds the size of the lining piece plus an extra ³⁄₈in (1cm), and the other piece one-third the size of the lining piece plus an extra ³⁄₈in (1cm)
- Two pieces of ⁵⁄₈-in (15-mm) wide tape, each long enough to wrap around your mug as many times as you want them to, then tie in a knot or bow
- Tape measure
- Fabric scissors
- Iron and ironing board
- Pins
- Sewing threads to match fabrics
- Sewing machine
- Hand-sewing needle

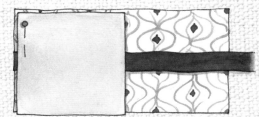

1 Lay the larger outer piece right side up. Lay one piece of tape across the middle of it, with a raw end against one of the short sides. Lay the other outer piece face down on top over the end of the tape, matching three raw edges.

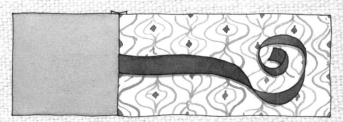

2 Taking a ³⁄₈-in (1-cm) seam allowance, sew the pieces together along the matched short edge. Press the seam open.

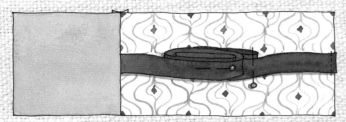

3 Baste (tack) one end of the other piece of tape to the free short edge of the larger outer piece, laying it across the middle, as before. Fold the free ends of both tapes up and pin them to the middle of the outer piece to keep them away from the edges.

4 Lay the lining piece face down on top of the outer piece, then lay the batting (wadding) on top of that, matching all raw edges.

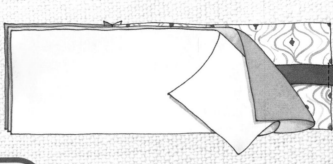

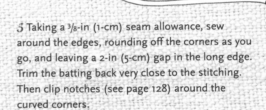

5 Taking a 3/8-in (1-cm) seam allowance, sew around the edges, rounding off the corners as you go, and leaving a 2-in (5-cm) gap in the long edge. Trim the batting back very close to the stitching. Then clip notches (see page 128) around the curved corners.

6 Turn the jacket right side out through the gap. Press it flat, pressing under the seam allowances across the gap, then ladder stitch (see page 131) the gap closed.

Find -YOUR- phone COZY

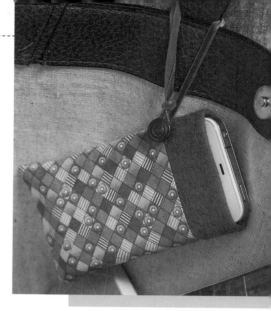

Your cell phone rings, you delve in your purse, and by the time you find your phone, whoever was calling you is long gone... again. Make a cozy that not only protects your cell phone but also keeps it easily retrievable in your purse. The lining of the cozy makes the cuff around the top edge, so make sure your lining and outer fabrics complement one another.

YOU'RE GOING TO NEED...

- Piece of thickish lining fabric measuring the circumference of your phone plus 1in (2.5cm), by the length of your phone plus 2in (5cm): I used boiled wool
- Piece of outer fabric measuring the circumference of your phone plus 1¼in (3cm), by the length of your phone: I used quilting cotton
- Piece of narrow ribbon measuring approximately 17½in (44cm) long: I used velvet ribbon: see Ribbon News, page 51
- Decorative button with a shank
- Fabric scissors
- Iron and ironing board
- Pins
- Sewing threads to match fabrics
- Sewing machine
- Hand-sewing needle

1 Right side in, fold the lining piece in half lengthwise and, taking a ³⁄₈in (1-cm) seam allowance, sew the side seam. Roll the seam to one side of the center back, then press the seam open and the lining tube flat. Leave the lining wrong side out. Do the same with the outer piece, rolling the seam to match that on the lining, so that when the two pieces are sewn together in Step 4, the seams are staggered.

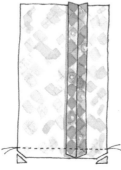

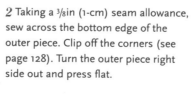

2 Taking a ³⁄₈in (1-cm) seam allowance, sew across the bottom edge of the outer piece. Clip off the corners (see page 128). Turn the outer piece right side out and press flat.

3 Fold the length of ribbon in half and, making sure it isn't twisted, baste (tack) the ends together. Then slip the loop into the lining tube and baste the ends to one side, aligned with the pressed fold.

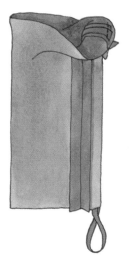

RIBBON NEWS

The ribbon needs to be narrow but sturdy—no thin silk, please. And it needs to be long enough that, when folded in half, it reaches from where you want your phone to hang inside your bag, up and around the handle, then back down to the phone, plus 2¼in (6cm).

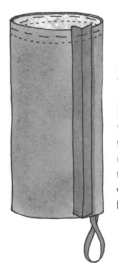

4 Right sides together, slip the outer piece inside the lining, matching the top raw edges. Baste the pieces together around the top edge, then, taking a 3/8-in (1-cm) seam allowance, sew them together. Sewing around such a tiny tube is a bit fiddly, but go slowly so that you can turn the tube smoothly. When I sewed over the ribbons, I reversed and then sewed forward again to make sure the ends were firmly stitched in. Remove the basting stitches.

5 Turn the whole thing right side out through the open end of the lining. Press the seam flat, then press under 3/8in (1cm) around the open end of the lining, making sure the lining is square to the outer. Whip stitch (see page 129) the open end closed.

6 Tuck the lining down inside the outer cozy, poking the corners into each other; you'll find a chopstick or a point turner useful for this. Press the top edge of the cozy flat. Sew on the button, next to where the ribbon comes out of the seam. Tie an overhand knot to make a small loop in the end of the ribbon, just large enough to slip over the button. Loop the ribbon around your bag handle and secure with the small end loop over the button.

YOU'RE GOING TO NEED...

- Wooden clothes hanger
- Two pieces of fabric at least 1¼in (3cm) wider than the clothes hanger and as deep as you want the cover to be: I used pieces of needlecord measuring 17 x 5½in (43 x 14cm)
- Trimming for the bottom edge of the cover (this is optional, but lovely...)
- Paper scissors and fabric scissors
- Paper, pen, and ruler for template
- Iron and ironing board
- Pins
- Sewing threads to match fabrics
- Sewing machine

Party TIME

Unless you have a very vibrant social life, there is going to be at least one glorious frock in your closet that only gets to see the light of day a few times a year. And when you do get it out, there are dust lines all along the shoulders so you have to take it to the cleaners... Solve the problem and make a cozy for your frock to keep it clean.

1 Draw a paper pattern for your party-frock cozy. Lay the hanger on a piece of paper and draw around the top edge, marking the position of the hook. Using a ruler, draw a line from the tip of one end of the hanger straight across to the tip of the other end. Then draw a line below that one at the depth you want the cozy to be. Draw straight lines down from the tips of the hanger to the bottom edge line, and that is your pattern.

To ensure that it is symmetrical, fold it in half at the mid-point (where the hook emerges), then cut it out through both layers. You need to add ⅝in (1.5cm) for seam allowances and ease around the top and sides, and ¾in (2cm) for a hem across the bottom edge, so either do this on the paper before you cut out the pattern, or add them when you cut out the fabric. Use the template to cut out two pieces of fabric.

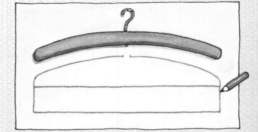

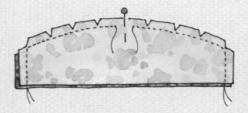

2 Pin the pieces right sides together and mark the mid-point (where the hook emerges) with a pin. Taking a ⅜-in (1-cm) seam allowance, sew up one side from the straight edge and around the curve, stopping ⅜in (1cm) before the mid-point pin. Reverse to secure the stitching. Repeat to sew up the other side of the cozy.

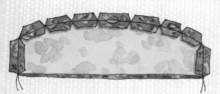

3 Clip notches (see page 128) in the seam allowances along the curves, and clip a wide notch at each end where the curve becomes a straight side, as shown. With the cozy flat, fold the upper layer seam allowances over and press them.

4 Then turn the cozy over and repeat the process, so that both layers of seam allowances are pressed toward the wrong side of the fabric.

5 Turn under and sew a double ³⁄₈-in (1-cm) hem around the bottom edge of the cozy. Then turn the cozy right side out and press it flat.

6 If you are going to add a trim to the bottom edge of the cozy, then you can sew it on and sew the hem at the same time.

EXTRA COZY

If you are making the cozy for a bulky garment, such as a winter coat, then you will need to add extra ease to the measurements so that the cozy fits over the thick fabric.

Keyed UP

Stop your keys from scratching and getting tangled with other stuff in your bag by keeping them in a cozy. An apple this size will hold a deadlock key; if you are only using a pin-tumbler key, then you can make your apple a bit smaller.

YOU'RE GOING TO NEED...

- Templates on page 133
- Two pieces of red felt measuring 4½in (12cm) square
- Two pieces of green felt measuring 3 x 2in (8 x 5cm)
- Stranded embroidery flosses (threads): see Floss Colors, below
- Approximately 10in (25cm) of ribbon
- Paper for templates
- Paper scissors and fabric scissors
- Pins
- Embroidery needle

FLOSS COLORS

I used four strands of floss to do the embroidery, two strands each of two different shades of red on the apple, and green on the leaves. It's a subtle effect, but it does make a difference.

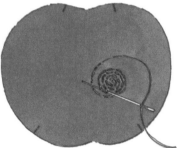

1 Trace the templates on page 133 and cut out. Cut out two apples from red felt and two leaves from green felt. Using chain stitch (see page 129), embroider a circle on what will be the front of the key cozy. Start in the middle and stitch in a tight spiral.

2 Place the two apples wrong sides together. Starting at the mark at one side of center top, sew the edges together using irregular blanket stitch (see page 130). When you get to the mark at one side of the center bottom, continue stitching, but through one layer of felt only, edging it rather than sewing the layers together.

3 Blanket stitch across to the mark on the other side of the center bottom, then stitch both edges together up to the mark on that side of the center top. Edge the felt around the top opening with blanket stitch and secure the floss by looping it through stitches on the inside of the apple. Finally, rejoin the floss on the inside of the apple at the bottom and blanket stitch across the raw edge of felt.

4 Knot the keys onto the middle of the length of ribbon. The ribbon needs to be long enough for the keys to hang below the apple when the ends protrude about ⅝in (1.5cm) above the top.

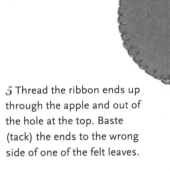

5 Thread the ribbon ends up through the apple and out of the hole at the top. Baste (tack) the ends to the wrong side of one of the felt leaves.

6 Position the second felt leaf shape on top, sandwiching the ribbon in between. Blanket stitch around the leaves, stitching the ribbon in place as you go. Remove the basting stitches. Simply slide the apple over the keys when you're not using them.

Tea's UP

You can't beat the all-time classic cozy; the tea cozy. But you can have some fun with it. This version is made from simple-to-sew wonky strippy patchwork, topped with perky pom-poms. It's an ideal project for using up scraps of lovely leftover fabrics.

1 Make a paper pattern as explained in How Much Fabric?, right. Cut two lining pieces and two batting (wadding) pieces using your paper pattern. I then used a lining piece as a template for the patchwork outer cozy, because I found it easier to pin in place, but you can use the paper pattern if you prefer.

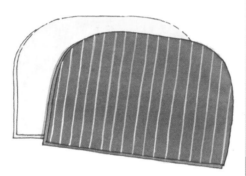

2 Taking ³⁄₈-in (1-cm) seam allowances, sew wonky strips together to make a rough rectangle that's a little larger all around than a lining piece. Cut the first strip, sew it right sides together to one edge of a larger piece of fabric, press the seam allowances open, and then cut the larger piece down to make a wonky strip the size you want. Continue in this way until the patchwork is the size you need. Make a second patchwork the same way: I made one with vertical strips and one with horizontal strips.

YOU'RE GOING TO NEED...

- Fabric and batting (wadding): see How Much Fabric?, below
- Pom-pom trimming
- Paper for template
- Paper scissors and fabric scissors
- Tape measure
- Iron and ironing board
- Pins
- Sewing threads to match fabrics
- Sewing machine with zipper foot
- Hand-sewing needle

HOW MUCH FABRIC?

- You need to start by making a paper pattern for your tea cozy. Measure right around your teapot, including the spout and handle, and divide that measurement in half. Measure from the top of the lid to the base. Add 1¹⁄₂in (4cm) ease and seam allowances to each measurement. Using these final measurements, draw a dome shape on paper. Cut it out, trace around it to draw another the same, then tape them together to make a muslin to try on your teapot. Adjust the fit if necessary.
- You'll need two pieces of lining fabric and two pieces of batting (wadding) large enough for your paper pattern, a selection of fabric pieces as wide or as tall as the pattern, and enough pom-pom trim to go around the top edge of the dome.

4 Lay one outer piece right side up. Starting on one side of the dome, ³/₄in (2cm) up from the straight bottom edge, baste (tack) the pom-pom trim to the patchwork, positioning the edge of the flat braid so that it is within the ³/₈in (1cm) seam allowance. Stop ³/₄in (2cm) before the straight edge on the other side of the dome.

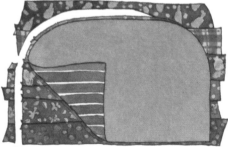

3 Pin the lining or paper pattern to the patchworks and use it as a template to cut out two outer tea cozies.

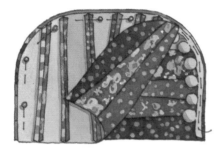

5 Lay the second patchwork piece right side down over the first, matching all raw edges. Pin the layers together. Sew the dome seam, taking a 3/8-in (1-cm) seam allowance and using a zipper foot so that the foot doesn't catch on the bobbles. Turn the outer cozy right side out and check that the bobbles look good. If anything needs fixing, do it now, unpicking and re-sewing parts of the seam if need be.

6 Pair up the lining pieces with the batting pieces, placing the batting on the wrong side of the lining. Treat these pieces as a single layer from now on. Pin the lining pieces right sides together and sew the dome seam, taking a 1/2-in (1.2-cm) seam allowance and leaving a 2-in (5-cm) gap at the center top: you can mark the position of this with pins before you sew. Trim the seam allowances down to 1/4in (5mm), except across the gap.

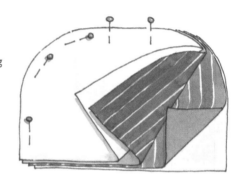

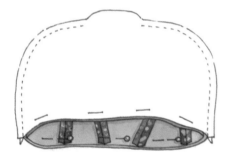

7 Slip the right-side out outer cozy into the inside-out lining, matching the bottom raw edges. Pin and then sew right around the bottom edge, taking a 3/8-in (1-cm) seam allowance.

8 Turn the cozy right side out through the gap in the lining,

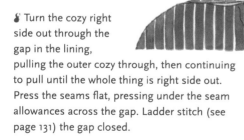

pulling the outer cozy through, then continuing to pull until the whole thing is right side out. Press the seams flat, pressing under the seam allowances across the gap. Ladder stitch (see page 131) the gap closed.

9 Tuck the lining inside the outer cozy and press the bottom edge. Topstitch around it, sewing 1/8in (2–3mm) in from the edge.

- Templates on page 137
- Hot water bottle: mine is 13 x 8in (33 x 20cm): see Fitted Up, below
- One piece of teal fleece measuring 12 x 12in (30 x 30cm), one piece measuring 7 x 12in (18 x 30cm), one piece measuring 6 x 12in (16 x 30cm), and two pieces measuring 2in (5cm) square
- Two pieces of pink fleece each measuring 8¾ x 12in (22 x 30cm)
- Two pieces of pale orange felt each measuring 2in (5cm) square
- 6in (15cm) of ⅝-in (1.5-cm) wide rick rack
- Scraps of felt, sequins, shisha mirrors, beads...
- About 16in (40cm) of two trims: I used jumbo and baby rick rack
- Two snap fasteners
- Paper for templates
- Paper scissors and fabric scissors
- Pins
- Sewing threads to match fabrics
- Perlé embroidery floss (thread)
- Hand-sewing needle
- Embroidery needle
- Sewing machine

HOT *monster*

• •

Delicious though the warmth of a hot water bottle is between chilly sheets, the clammy rubber isn't a welcome touch on one's toes. But the fleecy skin of your own personal monster is a whole other thing... I've given my monster rick-rack teeth and asymmetrical eyes, but you can customize yours however you want.

1 Enlarge the templates on page 137 by 200 percent. Fold the pieces of fleece in half. Pin the upper back template to the largest piece of teal fleece, matching the straight edge to the fold. Pin the head template to the middle-sized piece and the middle section template to the smaller piece, matching the straight edges to the folds. Pin the bottom template to one of the pink pieces, matching the straight edges to the fold. Cut all the pieces out, then pin the bottom template to the other pink piece of fleece and cut out a second bottom section. Cut two ears from the smallest pieces of teal fleece and two from felt, remembering to flip the template before cutting the second ear to produce a right and a left. Open all the folded pieces out to full width.

2 Turn under and baste (tack) a ⅜-in (1-cm) hem across the straight bottom edge of the head piece of fleece. Pin and then baste the 6-in (15-cm) piece of wide rick rack to the wrong side of the hem, positioning it centrally and so that one scalloped edge overlaps to show as teeth on the right side.

FITTED UP

If your hot water bottle is longer or shorter, adjust the length of the bottom template accordingly. If your bottle is wider or narrower, adjust all the templates by the required amount along the straight cut-on-the-fold edge.

3 Using perlé floss (thread), irregular blanket-stitch the hem (see page 130), sewing the rick rack in place at the same time. Remove the basting stitches.

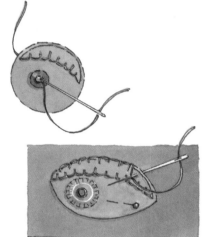

4 Make eyes for your monster using scraps of felt, sequins, shisha mirrors, beads... whatever you want. You can use the photograph as a guide, or create your own eyes. I cut one round and one almond eye from pale green felt. I cut eyelids from a different-color felt and stuck them to the eyes with fusible webbing, then I blanket-stitched along the lower edges of the lids, using perlé embroidery floss. I used a bead to hold a sequin to each eye, positioning it to one side of center, then sewed a shisha mirror frame over the sequin. Finally, I blanket-stitched the eyes to the head.

5 Turn under and sew a ³/₈-in (1-cm) hem along the top edge of the middle section. Then, taking a ³/₈-in (1-cm) seam allowance, sew a bottom section to the bottom edge of the middle section. Sew the other bottom section to the upper back section.

6 Arrange the trims on the lower half of the front body, pinning and/or basting them in place: I like to baste things, as I tend to stab myself on pins. Then sew the trims in place by hand or machine, whichever works best: I hand-sewed this rick rack on using pick stitch (see page 129).

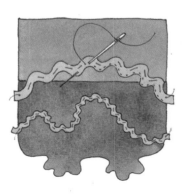

7 Right sides together, pin a felt ear to a fleece ear. Taking a ¼-in (5-mm) seam allowance, sew around the curved edge, leaving the bottom straight edge open. Trim the seam allowances down to ⅛in (2–3mm), then turn the ear right side out through the bottom edge. Repeat with the other ear pieces.

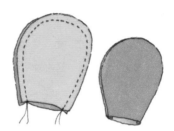

8 Felt side down, baste the ears to the head, matching the straight edge to the raw edge of the head. I didn't place my ears symmetrically, but you can if you prefer. Overlap the straight edge of the head template over the hemmed edge of the middle section by 1½in (4cm) and pin then baste it in place.

9 Right sides together, lay the back section over the front section, matching all edges and making sure the seams between the bottom and top sections match. Pin the layers together, then sew all around the edges, taking a ⅜-in (1-cm) seam allowance. Take out the basting stitches across the bottom of the head and turn the cozy right side out through the gap.

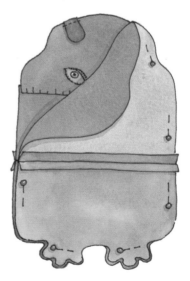

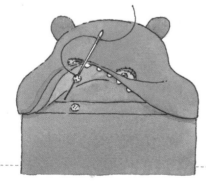

10 Sew on snap fasteners to close the cozy, sewing one half to the inside of the head section and the other half to the middle section: I sewed the head half to the back of each eye, sewing through the fleece only so that no stitches showed on the front.

Egged ON

When I acquired step-siblings, there were a few fundamentals to sort out. Mayonnaise or salad cream? George Clooney or Brad Pitt? Hendricks or Bombay Sapphire gin? (Don't fret, we were all grown-ups when our parents married...) Toasted soldiers or bread-and-butter dippers? As regards the latter, one thing we did all agree on was the need for eggs to be soft-boiled, so therefore you need a cozy to keep your egg at optimum temperature while you fiddle about getting more coffee. (In case you are wondering, I choose the first option in everything...)

1 Trace the template on page 132 and cut out. The template will fit an average-size egg and egg cup: you can make a paper muslin to check that it'll fit your preferred egg size and egg cup. Using the template, cut out two felt shapes. Using small, shallow stitches that don't go right through the felt, sew the pom-pom trimming to the wrong side of one felt piece, arranging it so the pom-poms protrude over the edge, as shown.

2 Using three strands of floss (thread) and irregular blanket stitch (see page 130), sew across the bottom edge of the felt piece. Do not fasten off the floss.

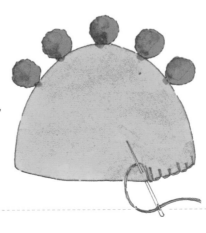

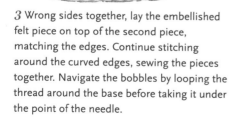

3 Wrong sides together, lay the embellished felt piece on top of the second piece, matching the edges. Continue stitching around the curved edges, sewing the pieces together. Navigate the bobbles by looping the thread around the base before taking it under the point of the needle.

4 Finish the cozy by stitching across the other bottom edge. Fasten off the floss by looping and knotting it around the legs of stitches on the inside of the cozy.

YOU'RE GOING TO NEED...

- Outer fabric, lining fabric, pocket fabric, and batting (wadding): see Size Matters, below
- Two zippers, both the width of the case: see Zipped Up, opposite
- Ribbon the width of the case
- Tape measure
- Fabric scissors
- Iron and ironing board
- Pins
- Sewing threads to match fabrics and ribbon
- Sewing machine with zipper foot
- Hand-sewing needle

SIZE MATTERS

- Measure the length, width, and depth of your tablet. Cut two pieces of outer fabric, two pieces of lining, and two pieces of batting each measuring the length plus twice the depth plus 1¼in (3cm), by the width plus twice the depth plus 1¼in (3cm).
- For example, my tablet is 5⅛in (13cm) wide, 8in (20cm) long, and ¼in (0.5cm) deep.
- So my pieces of lining and batting are 6⅞in (17cm) x 9½in (24cm).
  Width: 5⅛in (13cm) + ¼in (0.5cm) + ¼in (0.5cm) + 1¼in (3cm) = 6⅞in (17cm)
  Length: 8in (20cm) + ¼in (0.5cm) + ¼in (0.5cm) + 1¼in (3cm) = 9¾in (24cm)
- The pocket size needs to be the full width, but can be whatever depth suits you: my pocket is 6⅞in (17cm) x 6⅝in (16.5cm).
- This makes for a snug-fitting cover: if you want yours to be a little roomier, then add some extra ease all around.

TAKE YOUR
tablet (WITH YOU)

I resisted owning a tablet for ages: I had a desktop computer, a laptop, a smartphone, an mp3 player—how much kit could a girl possibly need? Then I spent a week away with someone who had a tablet with them, came home, and bought my own the next day. And now it's always in my bag: I read stuff on it, write notes and emails on the bus, wander the web when the fancy takes me. And because I take it everywhere, I wanted to make a practical, good-looking case for it. The instructions might seem a bit complicated, but you only need to sew straight lines, so just follow the steps carefully and all will be well.

1 Lay one zipper face down on the right side of the pocket piece, with one tape aligned with the top edge. Pin, then baste (tack) the tape in place. (I always prefer to baste zippers as I find it quicker and easier than sewing a pinned zipper and then taking out all the wobbly stitches and starting again.) Using a zipper foot, machine-sew the tape in place.

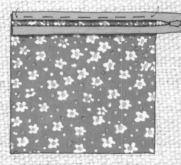

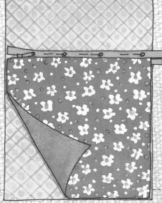

2 Close the zipper. Lay the pocket on the bag front, right side up, matching the lower raw edges, as shown. Pin then baste the other zipper tape to the bag front.

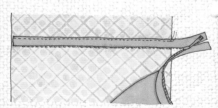

3 Open the zipper fully and sew the tape in place close to the outer edge.

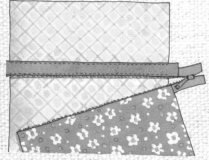

4 Baste the ribbon in place to cover the zipper tape on the right side. Then sew the ribbon on, sewing slowly and carefully as close to both ribbon edges as possible. This ribbon is decorative rather than functional, so if you are happy to have the zipper tape exposed, leave off the ribbon and sew the tape on close to the zipper teeth, as well as close to the outer edge.

5 Now shorten the zipper. Whip stitch (see page 129) firmly over the teeth at the edge of the case, then just cut the excess zipper off: do NOT use your best fabric scissors for this.

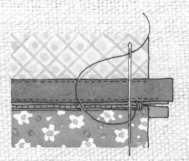

ZIPPED UP

The chances are that you won't find zippers the perfect length for your case. This can, in fact, be an advantage. Choose nylon-toothed zippers a bit longer than the case and push the sliders right down to the endstops, so that you don't have to negotiate them while sewing the tape on. You can alter the length once you have sewn the zippers on. I used invisible zippers for this project.

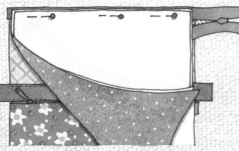

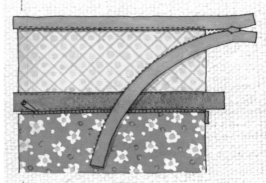

6 Lay the other zipper face down on the right side of the front case piece, with one tape aligned with the top edge. Pin, then baste, then sew the tape in place close to the teeth.

7 Pair up the lining pieces with the batting (wadding) pieces, placing the batting on the wrong side of the lining. Treat these pieces as a single layer from now on. Right side down, pin one piece of lining to the zipper tape you have just sewn to the front of the case. Sew it on, sewing close to the outer edge of the tape. Spacing the lining away from the teeth like this will prevent it from getting caught when the zipper is opened and closed.

8 Fold the lining over to the wrong side of the bag front, matching the raw edges. The free zipper tape will now be sticking up at the top of the case. Close the zipper.

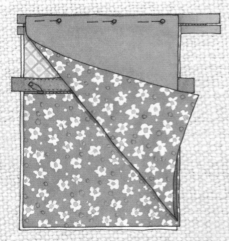

9 Right side down, pin, baste, then sew the back piece to the free tape, sewing close to the teeth.

10 Open the zipper fully. Lay the back piece out flat and lay the other lining piece right side down on top of it: you'll need to twist the zipper to do this. Sew it in place, sewing close to the outer edge of the tape, as before.

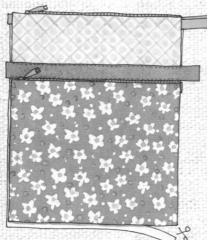

11 Close the top zipper and arrange all the layers so that the lining pieces are right sides together with the outer pieces right sides out on top of them. The lining will now be a bit too long, so trim off any protruding lining, trimming it back a tiny bit shorter than the outer fabric.

12 Open the top zipper halfway. Rearrange the layers so that the lining pieces are right sides together and so are the outer pieces, as shown. Taking a ³⁄₈-in (1-cm) seam allowance, sew right around the case, leaving a 2-in (5-cm) gap in the bottom of the lining. Trim off any protruding bits of zipper and ribbon. Zigzag the seam allowances and cut off the corners.

13 Turn the bag right side out through the gap in the lining, pulling the outer case through, then continuing to pull until the whole bag is right side out. Press the seams flat, pressing under the seam allowances across the gap. Ladder stitch (see page 131) the gap closed. Push the lining down inside the outer case.

CHAPTER 3

TO MAKE *gorgeous* THINGS I NEED...

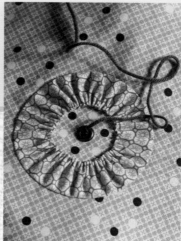

Get ORGANIZED

This is the perfect storage for a project that you have to keep setting aside because real life needs attention. The central section can hold yarns, fabric, whatever... and the little pockets around both sides will keep notebooks, pencils, scissors, needles, threads, trims... And then everything you need is just waiting there all together to be picked up when you have time to devote to it.

YOU'RE GOING TO NEED...

- Templates on pages 138–9
- Two pieces of sturdy outer fabric measuring 19 x 12in (48 x 30cm) and one piece measuring 11 x 6in (28 x 15cm): I used ticking
- Two pieces of lining fabric measuring 19 x 12in (48 x 30cm): I used quilting cotton
- One piece of sturdy lining measuring 11 x 6in (28 x 15cm): I used heavy cotton
- Two pieces of medium-weight pocket fabric measuring 19 x 6in (48 x 15cm): I used quilting cotton
- Two lengths of 1-in (2.5-cm) wide bias binding, 19in (48cm) long
- Paper for templates
- Paper scissors and fabric scissors
- Tape measure
- Iron and ironing board
- Pins
- Masking tape (optional)
- Sewing threads to match fabrics
- Sewing machine
- Hand-sewing needle

1 Enlarge the templates on pages 138–9 by 200 percent. Cut out one base piece and two side pieces from outer fabric: I had the stripe on my ticking running in different directions on each side piece. Cut two sides from lining fabric and one base from sturdy lining. Cut two pockets from the medium-weight fabric.

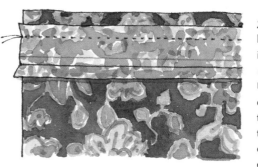

2 Press the bias binding in half lengthwise, but not exactly in half; have one edge ⅛in (2–3mm) above the other. Unfold the narrow half completely and, right sides together, pin the raw edge of the binding to the top edge of one pocket. The position of the edge of the binding will vary depending on how it was folded originally, but you need to pin it so that, when the binding is folded over the raw edge of the pocket, the pressed halfway fold runs along the top edge. Sew the binding in place, sewing along the original first fold.

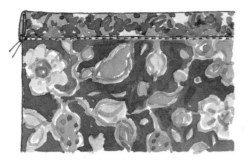

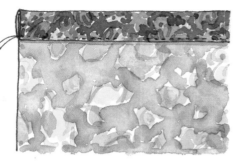

3 Fold the binding over the raw edge of the pocket to the back; the folded edge should just overlap the line of stitching made in Step 2. On the right side, stitch-in-the-ditch—

that is, sew along the seamline between the binding and the fabric—to complete the binding: the stitching should just catch the free folded edge of the binding on the back.

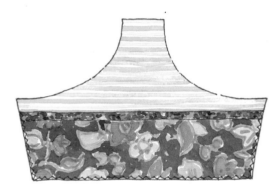

4 Lay a pocket piece right side up on the right side of a side piece, matching the raw edges. Set the sewing machine to a narrow zigzag and sew the layers together around the raw edges.

5 Divide the pockets into smaller sections with lines of sewing. Make them whatever sizes suit you and the projects you are going to use the bag for. You can use masking tape to mark out the lines. Stitch from the bottom to the top of the pocket. At the top of the pocket, take the threads through to the back and knot them very firmly. Repeat Steps 4 and 5 with the other side piece and pocket piece.

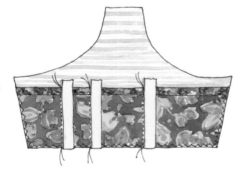

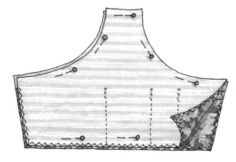

6 Pin the side pieces right sides together, matching the pocket tops carefully. Taking a 3/8-in (1-cm) seam allowance, sew the side seams. Press the seam allowances open.

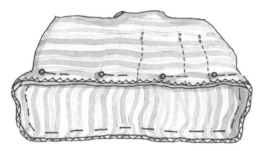

7 Right sides together, pin and then baste (tack) the base into the bag, easing it to fit around the curves. Taking a 3/8-in (1-cm) seam allowance, sew the seam. Turn the bag right side out and press the seam allowances upward toward the sides of the bag.

8 Make up the lining following Steps 6–7, but leave a 3-in (8-cm) gap in one side of the base. Leave the lining inside out.

9 Put the right-side out bag into the inside-out lining, matching the top raw edges. Sew around the edges, making one of the handles a tiny bit narrower than the other: leave the short straight ends of both handles open.

10 Turn the bag right side out through the gap in the lining, then ladder stitch (see page 131) the gap closed. Turn in 3/8in (1cm) of the end of the wider handle and press the fold. Tuck 3/8in (1cm) of the narrower handle inside the wider one and pin them together. Ladder stitch the ends together, stitching the outer layers, then the lining.

Go fish, FOR PENCILS

This felt fish will swallow a lot of pencils, plus your eraser, sharpener, and many other bits and bobs. He's entirely hand stitched, but it's easy stitching, and it will take less time than you might think.

1 Enlarge the templates on page 138 by 200 percent. Cut out one base piece and two back pieces, remembering to flip the upper template before cutting the second piece to produce a right and a left side.

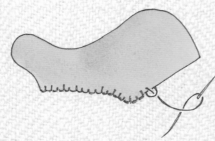

2 Using three strands of floss (thread) and irregular blanket stitch (see page 130), sew the two back pieces together from tail to mouth along the spine.

3 Open the fish back out flat. Using perlé floss and fly stitches (see page 130), sew on the buttons to make eyes. Sew a cross stitch (see page 131) into the center of each eye.

YOU'RE GOING TO NEED...

- Templates on page 138
- One piece of felt measuring 11 x 7in (28 x 18cm) and two pieces each measuring 11 x 6in (28 x 15cm)
- Stranded embroidery flosses (threads)
- Perlé embroidery floss: I used two different shades
- Two 4-hole buttons: I used two the same size, but slightly different colors
- 24in (60cm) of rick rack

- 6-in (15-cm) metal-toothed zipper
- Paper for templates
- Paper scissors and fabric scissors
- Pins
- Embroidery needle
- Sewing thread to match rick rack
- Hand-sewing needle

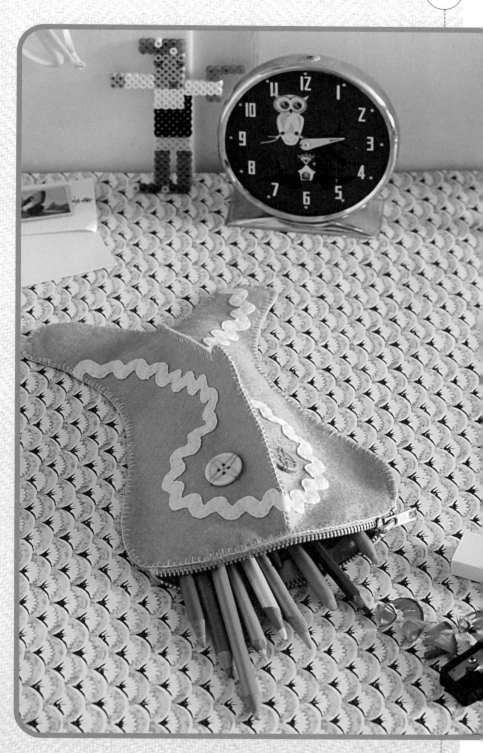

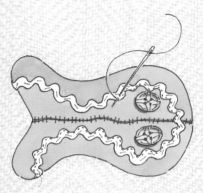

4 Baste (tack) the length of rick rack around the upper body, curving it gently. I didn't make the rick rack symmetrical on each side of the body, but you could if you wish. Using matching sewing thread and pick stitch (see page 129), sew the rick rack in place along each edge. Remove the basting stitches.

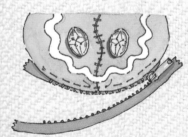

5 Baste one zipper tape across the mouth of the upper body. Find the mid-point of the tape and position that on the wrong side of the body, against the spine seam, then baste from the middle out to each edge. Fold the ends of the tapes back under the body and baste them out of the way.

6 Using three strands of floss and irregular blanket stitch, sew the zipper tape to the body. You need to sew close to the zipper teeth, but not so close that the stitching catches when the zipper is opened or closed: work a few stitches, then check that they are in a line where they don't catch before continuing to sew.

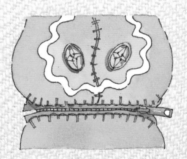

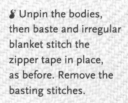

7 Close the zipper. Pin the upper body to the base, matching the raw edges. Then pin the free zipper tape to the base.

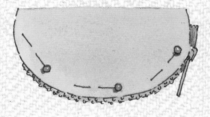

8 Unpin the bodies, then baste and irregular blanket stitch the zipper tape in place, as before. Remove the basting stitches.

9 Pin the bodies back together again and irregular blanket stitch all around the edges.

Safe SCISSORS

All keen sewists have at some point inadvertently stabbed themselves with their scissors, groping around to find them under a pile of fabric and encountering the points rather than the handles. This hanging scissor keeper allows you to stash your scissors somewhere you can find them easily, and safely. The small version lets you hang little scissors around your neck for über-convenience when embroidering. These keepers are entirely hand stitched, but irregular blanket stitch is both quick to work and very forgiving.

YOU'RE GOING TO NEED...

- Sturdy wool felt and medium-weight interfacing: see How Much Felt (And Interfacing)?, below
- ⅝-in (1.5-cm) diameter button
- Small decorative buttons
- Perlé embroidery floss (thread): I used a variegated floss
- Ribbon for loop
- Paper for templates
- Ruler and pencil
- Paper scissors and fabric scissors
- Fading fabric marker
- Iron and ironing board
- Pins
- Embroidery needle

1 You can make your pattern on paper, or do as I did and draw directly onto the wrong side of the felt with a fading fabric marker. Mark out a blunt-tipped triangle that is about three-quarters of the length of your scissors and wide enough across to accommodate the handles, plus a little extra to allow for the stitching. Cut two pieces of felt this shape.

HOW MUCH FELT (AND INTERFACING)?

- I made this keeper to fit my 8-in (21-cm) bent-handle dressmaking shears, and my triangles of felt measure 4⅜in (11cm) across the top and 6¼in (16cm) from top to tip. The piece of interfacing is ¼in (5mm) smaller all around than the triangle. The hanging loop is ¾ x 9in (2 x 23cm).
- The little keeper is for my 4-in (10-cm) embroidery scissors. The triangles of felt measure 2½in (6cm) across the top and 3in (8cm) from top to tip. The piece of interfacing is ¼in (5mm) smaller all around than the triangle. The neck loop is 29½in (75cm) of ⅜in (1cm) velvet ribbon.
- See Step 1 for how to make a pattern to fit your own scissors.

2 Using perlé floss (thread), work blanket-stitch wheels on the front of the keeper. This is optional, but they aren't difficult to do. Using the fabric marker, draw around the button in the position you want the wheel to be. Make dots on the edge of the button at the four main compass points, then space two more dots between each point. You can judge the points by eye; blanket-stitch wheels are very forgiving. Remove the button.

3 From the back, bring the needle up at one of the marked points. Pick a middle point for the wheel (this doesn't have to be the center of the circle; my middles were off to one side), and take the needle down through that, bringing it out at the next marked point to the right. Loop the floss under the tip of the needle and pull it through to make a stitch. Continue in this way right around the circle, inserting the needle at the same middle point each time. (See also page 130 for instructions for irregular blanket stitch.)

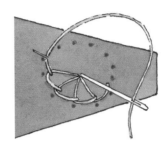

4 Secure the last stitch with a tiny straight stitch over the loop of the last blanket stitch. Fasten off the floss by looping and knotting it around the stitches on the back.

5 Using floss, sew a decorative button into the middle of each wheel. I used four-hole buttons and sewed them on with cross stitches (see page 131).

6 Iron the piece of interfacing onto the back of the embroidered front, so that the scissors don't get caught in the stitches.

7 Using perlé floss and irregular blanket stitch, stitch along both edges of the hanging loop strip.

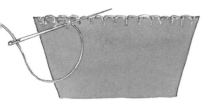

8 Using irregular blanket stitch, stitch across the top edge of the triangle that will be the back of the scissor keeper. Fasten off the floss by looping and knotting it around the legs of stitches on the back, as shown.

9 Fold the hanging loop in half, overlapping the ends so that the wrong side of one end lies on top of the right side of the other end. Sew it to the center back of the keeper, using a decorative button to hold the ends in place.

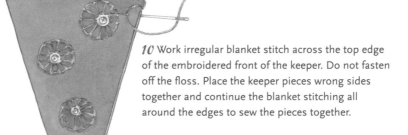

10 Work irregular blanket stitch across the top edge of the embroidered front of the keeper. Do not fasten off the floss. Place the keeper pieces wrong sides together and continue the blanket stitching all around the edges to sew the pieces together.

MY *mouse*

Pincushions obviously need to be practical, but there's no reason why they can't be whimsical, too. My mouse has a needlecord back—as that doesn't show pin marks as much as cotton fabric will—and he has mismatched eyes, because I liked them... His tail acts as a hanging loop to keep him stored out of mischief when he's not being useful.

YOU'RE GOING TO NEED...

- Templates on page 134
- One piece of nose fabric measuring 3 x 3½in (8 x 9cm), one piece of base fabric measuring 5½ x 8in (14 x 20cm), four pieces of ear fabric measuring 2½in (6cm) square, and one piece of tail fabric measuring 2 x 8in (5 x 20cm): I used quilting cotton
- One piece of back fabric measuring 6¾ x 6in (17 x 15cm): I used needlecord
- Polyester toy filling
- Small buttons and/or beads for eyes and button or pom-pom for nose: see Step 9
- Paper for templates
- Paper scissors and fabric scissors
- Iron and ironing board
- Pins
- Sewing threads to match fabrics
- Sewing machine

1 Trace the templates on page 134 and cut out. Cut out one nose piece, one base piece, four ear pieces, and one back piece. Make pleats in the back piece following the marks on the template; baste (tack) the pleats in place either side of the ³/₈-in (1-cm) seam allowance.

2 Pin two ear pieces right sides together. Taking a ³/₈-in (1-cm) seam allowance, sew around the curve. Trim the seam allowances and clip notches (see page 128) around the curves. Turn the ear right side out and press it flat. Pleat the straight edge and baste across, ³/₈in (1cm) from the raw edge. Repeat to make a second ear, pleating it to mirror the first one.

3 Pin the ears to the top edge of the right side of the back piece, positioning them ³/₈in (1cm) apart. Baste them in place.

4 Right sides together, pin the nose piece to the top edge of the back piece, over the ears. Taking a ³⁄₈-in (1-cm) seam allowance, sew the seam. Press the seam allowances toward the nose.

5 Right side in, fold the tail strip in half lengthwise. Taking a ³⁄₈-in (1-cm) seam allowance, sew the long edge. Turn the tube right side out (see page 128). With the seam along one edge, press the tube flat.

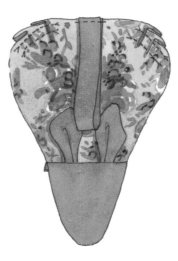

6 Fold the tail in half and baste the ends to the bottom edge of the right side of the back, centering it. Match the ends of the loop to the raw edge of the back and make sure that the loop is square to the edge.

7 Right sides together, pin the base piece over the mouse back, matching the raw edges all around. Taking a 3/8-in (1-cm) seam allowance, sew the seam, leaving a 2-in (5-cm) gap in one side. Zigzag and trim the seam allowances, and clip notches (see page 128) around the curves.

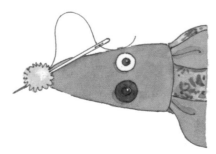

8 Turn the mouse right side out through the gap and carefully press the seam, pressing under the seam allowances across the gap. Stuff the mouse as firmly as possible with toy filling. Ladder stitch the gap closed (see page 131).

9 Sew on the eyes and nose. I used different-colored buttons topped with beads for eyes and a pom-pom from furnishing trim for the nose.

Knitting KNOW-HOW

I LOVE this yarn carrier; it's just so very useful. And so very easy to make. Not only does it let me knit wherever I am, but it also stops my ball of yarn tumbling across the floor to be pursued by pets. If you are color knitting, then you can put two balls of yarn in, one at each end, and the carrier will help prevent horrible tangles. This version is large enough to hold a 3½oz (100g) ball of yarn.

YOU'RE GOING TO NEED...

- Piece of fabric measuring 15 x 13½in (38 x 34cm) and strip measuring 3 x 16in (8 x 40cm): I used cotton fabric
- 2 lengths of cord, each 14½in (36cm) long
- Piece of heavyweight fusible interfacing measuring 14½ x 7in (36 x 18cm)
- Cord elastic, 16in (40cm)
- 1½-in (3.5-cm) diameter button
- Fabric scissors
- Iron and ironing board
- Pins
- Safety pin or bodkin
- Sewing threads to match fabrics
- Sewing machine with zipper foot

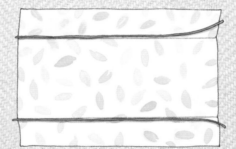

1 Press under a 2¾-in (7-cm) hem along each long edge of the large piece of fabric. Open the hems out and lay a length of cord along each fold.

2 Fold the fabric over the cord and pin the layers together close to the cord. Using a zipper foot, sew as close to the cord as possible to encase it in a fabric channel. Leave the ends of the cord poking out for the time being.

3 Iron the piece of fusible interfacing to the wrong side of the fabric, between the cord channels. Center it from side to side so that there is 3/8in (1cm) of fabric protruding at each end. Press under a 1/4-in (5-mm) and then a 3/8-in (1-cm) hem, along each long edge.

4 Right side in, fold the handle strip in half lengthwise. Taking a 3/8-in (1-cm) seam allowance, sew the long edge. Turn the tube right side out (see page 128). With the seam along one edge, press the tube flat. Turn in and press 3/8in (1cm) at each end.

5 Fold the handle in half widthwise and pin the ends to the right side of the main piece, positioning them 1½in (3.5cm) down from one cord channel, and 4¾in (12cm) from one edge. Sew the ends in place, sewing a small square of stitches across them through all three layers of fabric.

6 Open out the pressed hems. Right side in, pin the short edges of the fabric together, matching the ends of the cord carefully: I basted (tacked) across these for accuracy. Taking a ⅜-in (1-cm) seam allowance, sew the side seam. Zigzag the seam allowances together and trim them, then press them to one side.

7 Re-fold the hems and sew them in place, sewing very close to the folded edge and leaving a small gap in the stitching on each hem.

❧ Cut the cord elastic in half. Using a safety pin or bodkin, thread one length of cord elastic through each hem. At the back of the holder (the end without the handle), pull the elastic as tight as possible and knot the ends firmly: put in a few stitches if necessary to hold the knot secure. At the other end, make the elastic tight enough to allow a ball of yarn to be pushed through the opening. Knot and sew the ends as before. Turn the holder right side out.

9 Sew on the button over the ends of the handle as a finishing touch. Pull the working end out of the center of the ball of yarn, then push the ball into the carrier, loop the handle over your wrist, and knit on the move!

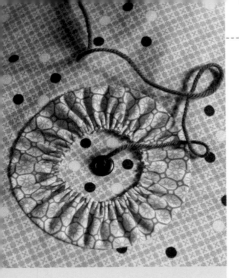

LOVELY *colors*

I've never mastered knitting Fair Isle with both hands; I go for the both-yarns-in-the-right-hand technique, and just loop the appropriate yarn over the needle. This works perfectly well as regards gauge (tension), but twists the two yarns around one another with every color change, resulting in what quickly become horrible tangles. Even if you can work with both hands, keeping the two yarns separate is always a plus; and this bag does exactly that. There's a central divider between the two balls of yarn, and an eyelet in each side of the bag to thread the strands through and so keep them apart. Plus, you can make the bag big enough to store your knitting. And there's a loop handle to carry it or hang it up from. Ideal!

YOU'RE GOING TO NEED...

- Two pieces of fabric measuring 12 x 15in (30 x 38cm) for the outer bag
- One piece of fabric measuring 12½ x 25in (32 x 64cm) and one piece of fusible webbing measuring 12½in (32cm) square for the divider
- One piece of fabric measuring 2 x 15in (5 x 38cm) for the carrying/hanging loop
- Two pieces of fabric measuring 6in (15cm) square and two pieces of fabric and of fusible webbing measuring 3½in (9cm) square for the yo-yos
- Charm for zipper pull (optional)
- 10in (25cm) zipper
- Tape measure
- Small plate
- Fabric marker
- Fabric scissors
- Ruler
- Iron and ironing board
- Pins
- Compasses
- Sewing threads to match fabrics
- Sewing machine with zipper foot
- Eyelet kit
- Hand-sewing needle

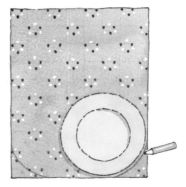

1 Round off what will be the two bottom corners of the outer bag: I drew around a plate with the fabric marker to get a smooth curve. Cut out following the marked lines.

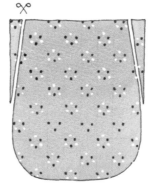

2 Using the ruler and fabric marker, narrow the top edge of the bag to measure 10in (25cm) wide, as shown.

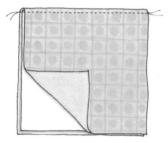

3 Right side out, press the divider piece of fabric in half widthwise. Slip the fusible webbing between the layers and iron again to fuse them together. Topstitch the folded (top) edge, stitching ⅛in (2–3mm) in from the edge.

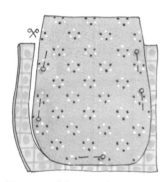

4 Lay one of the outer bag pieces on top of the divider, making sure the folded edge of the divider and the top edge of the bag are parallel, with the bag extending about 2½in (6cm) above the top of the divider. Use the bag piece as a template to cut out the divider.

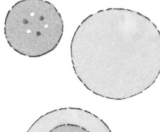

5 Using compasses, draw a 5¾-in (14.5-cm) circle on each larger piece of fabric for the yo-yos. Draw two 3¼-in (8.5-cm) circles on the paper backing of the pieces of fusible webbing, iron them onto the back of the smaller pieces of fabric, then cut out all the circles (two large and two small). Iron the smaller circles onto the wrong side of the larger ones, positioning them centrally.

6 Turn under a narrow hem to the wrong side on the edge of each larger circle and, starting with a knot on the wrong side, work a row of small running stitches around the edge, turning under the hem all around as you sew. Do not fasten off the thread, but leave a short tail protruding from the wrong side.

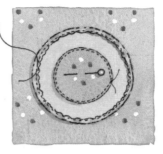

7 Position a yo-yo on the right side of each bag piece. They can be wherever you like: I put one low down on one side and the other high up on the other side. Pin them in place through the middle circle. Sewing slowly and carefully, sew around the edge of the middle circle, sewing it to the bag.

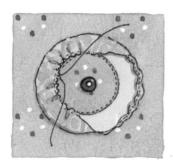

8 Following the instructions on the eyelet kit, insert an eyelet into the center of each yo-yo, going through all layers. Pull on the tail of thread and the starting knot to gather up the outer edge of each yo-yo. You want to gather them as tightly as possible, while keeping the middle circle lying flat. Knot the threads securely.

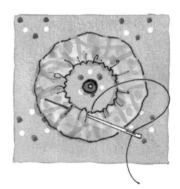

9 Hand sew the gathered edge of each yo-yo down, using small stitches hidden in the troughs of the gathers. Slip the needle between the bag fabric and the yo-yo to avoid loops of thread on the inside of the bag.

10 Lay one bag piece right side down and lay the divider on top of it, matching the raw edges. Zigzag stitch the layers together around the edge.

11 Right side in, fold the loop strip in half lengthwise. Taking a 3/8-in (1-cm) seam allowance, sew the long edge. Turn the tube right side out (see page 128). With the seam along one edge, press the tube flat.

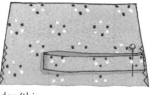

12 Fold the loop in half, matching the raw ends, and pin them square to the edge of the bag, just below the top of the divider (this means that the handle will emerge from the strongest part of the bag).

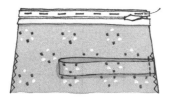

13 Add a charm to the zipper pull, if you wish (see Absolutely Charming, right). Lay the zipper face down on the right side of one bag piece, with one tape aligned with the top edge. Pin then baste (tack) the tape in place. (I always prefer to baste zippers, as I find it quicker and easier than sewing a pinned zipper and then taking out all the wobbly stitches and starting again.)

ABSOLUTELY CHARMING

You can, if you wish (and I did), replace the zipper pull with a charm. Use pliers to cut off the existing pull and thread a jump ring through the loop on the zipper to hang the charm from.

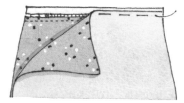

14 Lay the bag piece and zipper right side up. Place the other bag piece right side down on top, aligning the free tape with the top edge. Baste the tape to the bag piece. Using a zipper foot, machine-sew the zipper to each bag piece, stitching close to the teeth. Remove the basting stitches and press the seams.

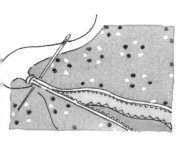

15 Trim the seam allowances to a little less than the width of the zipper tape. Zigzag stitch the tapes to the seam allowances to neaten them. At the open end of the zipper, whip stitch (see page 129) the tapes together.

16 Undo the zipper halfway. Pin the bag pieces right sides together, matching the raw edges. Sew all around the edges. Trim and zigzag or serge (overlock) the seam allowances to neaten them. Turn the bag right side out through the zipper and press the seam flat.

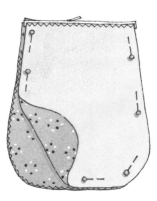

Sewn UP

• •

FITTED UP

- Measure the length of your sewing machine, and right over it from back to front, from the table top on one side to the table top on the other. Add ³⁄₈in (1cm) seam allowances all around and cut two rectangles of fabric—a lining and an outer—to these measurements. It's good if one piece has some body to it, so for the flowery pinafore I used a thin, drapey wool fabric with a stiff calico as the lining. The tweed fabric is quite thick, so I used cotton curtain lining to line that. I cut a pocket piece the length of the machine by 4³⁄₈in (11cm), though this is optional. If you make the pocket, then you need a piece of bias binding the length of the machine. You don't need to untie the pinafore every time you undress the machine: tie it carefully the first time, then just slip it on and off.

A dust cover for your sewing machine is always a good idea, and if, like me, you have more than one machine (three sewing machines, a serger, and an embellisher...), then how fab to have a coordinated set of covers: it makes your machine collection look more intentional (instead of impulsive...). Fitted covers are certainly practical—and protective if your machine is going traveling—but they can be a pain to fit neatly to the lumps and bumps of a sewing machine. For machines that live at home you only need one of these easy-to-make dust covers, which my grandma always used to refer to as her machine's "pinafore." The pockets make useful stashes for bits of sewing kit that live with the machine.

1 Fold the bias binding over the top edge of the pocket and pin it in place. Set the sewing machine to a medium zigzag stitch and sew the binding in place. Press under the bound edge to the wrong side by ³⁄₈in (1cm) and sew the hem using straight stitch.

2 Lay the cover outer fabric flat and right side up. Lay the pocket piece right side up against the bottom edge of what will be the front, matching the raw edges, as shown. Pin the layers together.

3 Mark divisions in the pocket with strips of masking tape, making them whatever sizes suit you. Starting at the bottom edge, sew along an edge of each strip of tape to make the pockets, stopping sewing at the top of the pocket. Leave long tails of thread. Thread a tail into a hand-sewing needle and make a few reinforcing backstitches at the top of each line of sewing, then take the tails through to the back and tie off the threads securely.

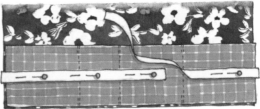

4 Cut the linen tape into four equal-sized pieces. Pin one end of a piece of tape to each edge of the pocket. The height you pin them at depends on your machine; you want the tapes to tie across the end of the free arm. Pin the other two pieces of tape to the other end of the pinafore, at the same height from the edge as the first two pieces. Pin the lengths to the fabric to keep them out of the way of the stitching.

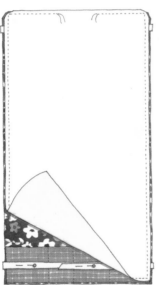

5 Right side down, lay the lining piece on top of the outer fabric, matching all raw edges. Taking a ³⁄₈-in (1-cm) seam allowance, sew all around the edges, leaving a 3-in (8-cm) gap in the middle of the back bottom edge. Clip all the corners, as shown at the top of the illustration.

6 Turn the cover right side out through the gap. Press it flat, pressing under the seam allowances across the gap. Ladder stitch (see page 131) the gap closed.

Rolled UP

In my book *Sewlicious*, I made a simple knitting-needle roll: this is the über-version. It'll hold a whole load of stuff for knitting and crochet, keeping it all portable and to hand. And this is still a very quick and easy make.

YOU'RE GOING TO NEED...

- One piece of medium-weight fabric measuring 16 x 4⅜in (40 x 11cm), one piece measuring 16 x 7½in (40 x 19cm), one piece measuring 16 x 10⅝in (40 x 27cm), and two pieces measuring 16 x 16in (40 x 40cm): I used ticking throughout
- 35in (90cm) of narrow tape: I used linen tape
- Tape measure
- Fabric scissors
- Iron and ironing board
- Pins
- Masking tape
- Sewing threads to match fabrics
- Sewing machine
- Hand-sewing needle

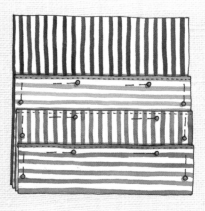

1 Press under and sew a double ⅜-in (1-cm) hem along one long straight edge of the three smaller pieces of fabric. Lay one of the largest pieces of fabric flat and right side up. Right side up, stack the three hemmed pieces on top, matching the bottom raw edges, as shown. Pin the layers together.

2 Decide on the spacing for the pockets. You can lay out equipment you want the roll to hold and then mark the divisions with strips of masking tape.

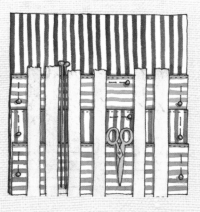

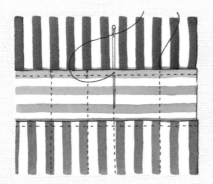

3 Starting at the bottom edge, sew along an edge of each strip of tape to make the pockets (I sewed along the left-hand edge of each piece of tape), stopping sewing at the top of the deepest pocket. Leave long tails of thread. Thread a tail into a hand-sewing needle and make a few reinforcing backstitches at the top of each line of sewing, then take the tails through to the back and tie off the threads securely.

4 Fold the length of linen tape in half and baste the fold to the right-hand side of one edge of the roll, level with the top of the middle row of pockets. Fold and pin the tape to the roll to keep it out of the way of the stitching.

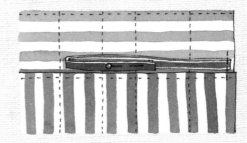

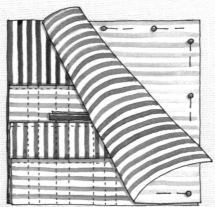

5 Lay the remaining large piece of fabric right side down over the pocket piece, matching all raw edges. Pin the layers together all around. Sew the seam, taking a ³⁄₈-in (1-cm) seam allowance and leaving a 3-in (8-cm) gap in one side edge, above the deepest pocket.

6 Turn the roll right side out through the gap and press it flat, pressing under the seam allowances across the gap. Use ladder stitch (page 131) to sew the gap closed.

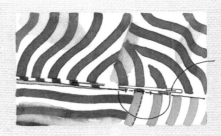

PINNED *up*

YOU'RE GOING TO NEED...

- Two pieces of fabric and one piece of heavyweight interfacing, each measuring 10½ x 6⅛in (26.5 x 15.5cm) for the thread bag: I used needlecord fabric throughout
- Two pieces of fabric measuring 8 x 10in (20 x 25cm) for the base
- One piece of fabric measuring 2¾ x 4¼in (7 x 10.5cm) for the pocket
- One piece of fabric measuring 1¾ x 12in (4.5 x 30cm) for the loop
- Two pieces of fabric measuring 10 x 4in (25 x 10cm) for the pincushion
- Button
- Polyester toy filling
- Tape measure
- Fabric scissors
- Iron and ironing board
- Pins
- Sewing threads to match fabrics
- Sewing machine
- Fabric marker
- Small plate
- Hand-sewing needle
- Two door hinges, or something else flat and heavy to use as a weight for the pincushion

This really is the most amazingly useful piece of kit, especially if, like me, you love hand-sewing in front of a good movie on the television. Hang this pincushion over the arm of your chair, and you have pins and scissors to hand, plus a repository for all the scraps of thread that otherwise find their way onto the floor. Or you can stash small tools and notions in the bag. It's quite a long project, as there are various elements to make, but nothing is complicated.

1 Iron the interfacing onto the back of the inner thread bag. Fold the piece in half widthwise and, taking a ⅜-in (1-cm) seam allowance, sew the seam. Don't interface the outer bag, but sew it in the same way. Trim the seam allowances to half their width on the inner. Roll the seam allowances to just off center back— so that when the two pieces are put together the seams are staggered— and press them open.

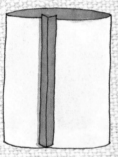
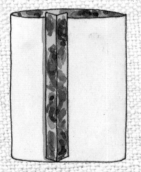

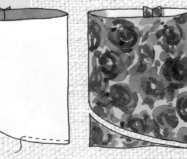

2 Turn the outer bag right side out and cut the bottom edge into a curve, curving down from left to right. Leave the inner bag wrong side out, and use the outer bag as a template to cut it to the same shape. Turn the outer bag wrong side out and, taking a ⅜-in (1-cm) seam allowance, sew the curved base. Then turn it right side out again. Sew the curved seam of the inner bag, but leave a 2-in (5-cm) gap in the middle of the seam.

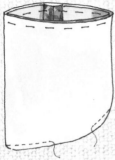

3 Slip the outer bag into the inner, so the right sides are together. Baste and then sew the layers together around the top edge, taking a ³⁄₈-in (1-cm) seam allowance.

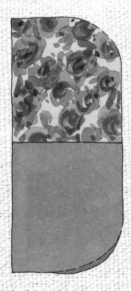

4 Turn the bag right side out through the gap in the lining, pulling the outer bag through, then continuing to pull until the whole piece is right side out. Press it flat, pressing under the seam allowances across the gap. Ladder stitch (see page 131) the gap closed.

5 Turn the inner bag down inside the outer, pushing out the corner and curve smoothly. Topstitch around the top edge of the bag, sewing ¹⁄₈in (2–3mm) in from the edge. Sew the button to the center back of the inner bag, ⁵⁄₈in (1.5cm) down from the top edge.

6 Zigzag or serge (overlock) one short edge of the pocket piece. Press under a ³⁄₈-in (1-cm) hem on that edge. Sewing ³⁄₈in (1cm) in from each raw side edge, sew across the hem, as shown. Clip off the corners of the hem.

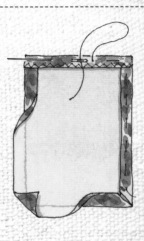

7 Turn the hem right side out and press it flat. Press under and baste (tack) a ³⁄₈-in (1-cm) hem all around the pocket, mitering the two bottom corners.

8 Right side in, fold the loop strip in half lengthwise. Taking a ³⁄₈-in (1-cm) seam allowance, sew the long edge. Turn the tube right side out (see page 128). With the seam along one edge, press the tube flat.

9 Round off the left-hand bottom corner of the base pieces: I drew around a small plate. Position the pocket on the right side of a base piece, 1¹⁄₄in (3cm) in from both the side and the bottom edges of the square right-hand bottom corner. Topstitch it in place, then take out the basting stitches. Fold the loop in half, overlapping the ends so that the wrong side of one end lies on top of the right side of the other end, and baste the raw edges to the top edge of the base, 1¹⁄₂in (4cm) from the left-hand edge. Pin the length of the loop to the base to keep it out of the way of the stitching.

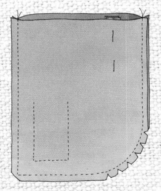

10 Lay the other base piece right side down on top of the first one, matching all raw edges. Taking a ³⁄₈-in (1-cm) seam allowance, sew all around the edges, but leave the top straight edge open. Clip the curves (see page 128) and turn the base right side out. Press the seams flat.

11 Lay one pincushion piece flat, right side up. Lay the base right side down centered on top of it, matching the open raw edge with the far edge of the pincushion piece, as shown. Baste the edges together. Lay the other pincushion piece right side down on top of the first, matching all edges. Pin the layers together along the top edge.

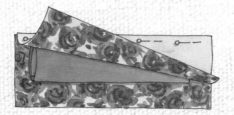

12 Roll the base up as tightly as possible and tuck it in between the pincushion pieces. Pin the pincushion pieces together all around, enclosing the rolled-up base.

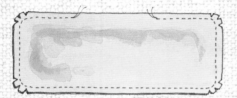

13 Taking a ⅜-in (1-cm) seam allowance, sew the pincushion seams, making the corners gently rounded and leaving a 3-in (8-cm) gap in the middle of the edge the base is basted to. Clip the curves.

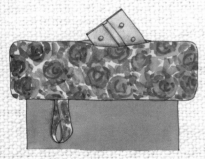

14 Turn the pincushion right side out through the gap, unrolling the base piece. Press everything, apart from the loop, flat, pressing under the seam allowances across the gap. Fold the pincushion forward over the top edge of the base, into the position it will sit in when finished. Slip the door hinges in through the gap, positioning them to lie flat along the underside of the pincushion.

15 Fill the pincushion with plenty of stuffing, pushing it in on top of the hinges until the pincushion is firm. Ladder stitch (see page 131) the gap closed. Button the bag onto the loop.

CHAPTER 4

TO *chill*

I NEED...

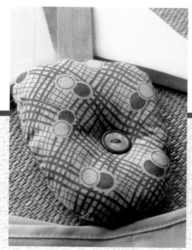

Scentilicious

Lavender bags smell delicious, but often look embarrassingly twee. Why? I've no idea; there's no need for it. Make your own from scraps of your favorite fabrics, and give them little loops so you can put them on clothes hangers and make your whole closet scentilicious. The buttons help to make the lavender bag pleasingly firm, but you don't have to add them.

1 Place the fabrics right sides together and cut out the shape you want your bag to be, remembering to cut it about 3/8in (1cm) larger all around to allow for seam allowances. If you prefer, you can make a paper template and draw around that.

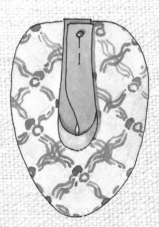

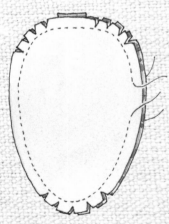

2 Fold the tape in half, overlapping the ends so that the right side of one end lies on top of the wrong side of the other end. Pin the folded tape to the right side of the front of the bag, matching the raw ends to the top edge.

3 Lay the other piece of fabric right side down on top of the first piece, with the tape in between. Taking a 3/8in (1-cm) seam allowance, sew around the edges, leaving a small gap in one side. Cut notches in the seam allowances (see page 128) around any curves.

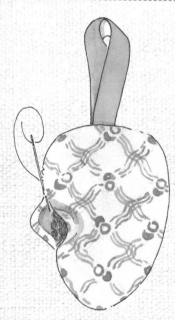

4 Turn the bag right side out through the gap and press it flat. Fill the bag with dried lavender, then ladder stitch (see page 131) the gap closed.

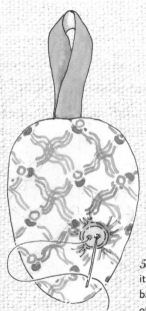

5 Thread the hand-sewing needle with a long length of thread, double it, and knot the ends. From the back, take the needle right through the bag, then thread on the decorative button. Go back down through the other hole in the button and right through to the back of the bag, then thread on the plain button. Pull the thread tight. Go back and forth through both buttons a few times, then secure the thread by looping and knotting it under the button on the back.

I ♥ books

While I understand the practical advantages of an e-reader (especially when trying to read *Wolf Hall* or *The Goldfinch* in bed without incurring muscle strain or a bruised face), I don't find them conducive to a good reading experience. For me, it has to be an actual book every time. So, I show my love for books large and small with a quick-to-make and oh-so-practical bookmark that just slips over the corner of your page.

YOU'RE GOING TO NEED...

- Template on page 133
- Two pieces of felt measuring 3½ x 3in (9 x 8cm)
- Paper for templates
- Paper scissors and fabric scissors
- Fading fabric marker
- Embroidery needle
- Stranded embroidery floss (thread)

1 Trace the template on page 133 and cut out. Cut out two hearts from felt and transfer the marks from the template.

2 Starting at the mark on one side, and using two strands of floss (thread), blanket stitch (see page 130) across the curves of one heart to the mark on the other side. Finish the floss on the back of the heart.

3 Do the same on the other heart, but don't finish off the floss. Place the two hearts wrong sides together, then continue blanket stitching to sew both hearts together. Finish the stitching on the inside when you get to the start of the single-layer stitching.

Mat MATE

I hate exercise: there, I've admitted it. The only exception to this rule is ashtanga yoga, which I rather like. However, the mat is ugly, so I made a good-looking cover-up for mine for when we are out in public. This is a super-simple, quick make. The bag will hold a mat measuring 23½ x 68in (60 x 173cm).

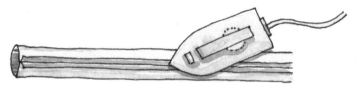

1 Right side in, fold the handle strip in half lengthwise. Taking a ⅜in (1-cm) seam allowance, sew the seam. Press the seam allowance open, then turn the tube right side out (see page 128). Roll the seam to the center back and press the handle flat.

2 Mark the mid-point on one long edge of the bag piece of fabric. Measure 10in (25cm) along the edge from that point and pin one end of the handle to the right side of the piece, matching the raw edges and with the seam facing down. Measure 10in (25cm) in the other direction from the mid-point, and pin the other end of the handle in place, making sure the handle isn't twisted.

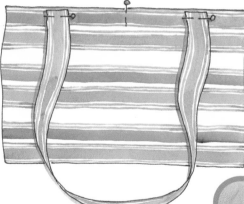

YOU'RE GOING TO NEED...

- Piece of sturdy fabric measuring 20 x 31in (50 x 79cm) for bag: I used ticking
- Strip measuring 39 x 4¾in (100 x 12cm) for handle: I used the same ticking as for the bag
- Two pieces of cord each measuring 30in (75cm) long
- Tape measure
- Fabric scissors
- Iron and ironing board
- Pins
- Sewing threads to match fabrics
- Sewing machine

3 Right side in, fold the bag piece in half lengthwise and pin the long edges together, making sure the loop of the handle is tucked away from the stitching line. Taking a 3/8-in (1-cm) seam allowance, sew 13/8in (3.5cm) at the top of the seam, reversing at each end to secure the stitching. Leave a 3/8in (1-cm) gap, then sew the seam, reversing then going forward again over the ends of the handles as you get to them. Stop sewing 11/2in (4.5cm) before the end of the seam, leave a 3/8in (1-cm) gap, then sew the last 13/8in (3.5cm) of the seam. Zigzag or serge (overlock) the seam allowances and press them open.

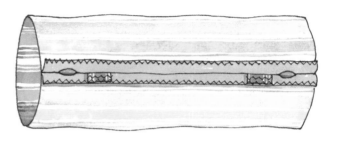

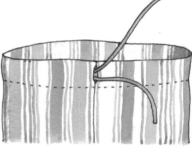

4 Around each end of the tube, press under 3/8in (1cm), then 3/4in (2cm). Sew the hems, sewing very close to the lower folded edge. Turn the tube right side out. Thread a piece of cord through each channel, threading it through the gap in the side seam, and draw the ends tight.

Doubled UP

This is my preferred style of oven glove: I don't like two separate mittens as I always manage to drop one just after I've opened the oven door. You can buy special heat-resistant batting (wadding), and choosing washable fabrics will make your gloves practical as well as lovely to look at.

1 Pin the 8in (20cm) squares of fabric and batting (wadding) together in pairs. Draw around the plate, or use compasses, to round off two adjacent corners of each square. Also round off the corners at both ends of the long pieces of fabric and batting. Trim off the corners following the curved line.

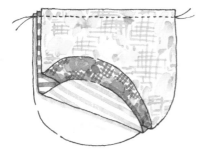

2 Lay a rounded square of sturdy fabric right side up on a rounded square of batting and then lay a rounded square of decorative fabric right side down on top of the sturdy fabric. Pin the layers together and, taking a 3/8-in (1-cm) seam allowance, sew across the top straight edge.

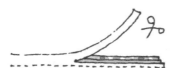

3 Trim the seam allowance of the batting down to just 1/8in (2–3mm) from the stitching.

YOU'RE GOING TO NEED...

- Two pieces of sturdy fabric and one piece of heat-resistant batting (wadding) measuring 8 x 33½in (20 x 85cm) and two pieces of sturdy fabric and of heat-resistant batting measuring 8in (20cm) square: I used ticking for the fabric
- Two pieces of decorative fabric measuring 8in (20cm) square for the front of the mitts, and one piece measuring 5 x 7in (5 x 18cm) for the loop: I used quilting cotton
- Tape measure
- Fading fabric marker
- 8-in (20-cm) diameter plate, or compasses
- Fabric scissors
- Iron and ironing board
- Pins
- Sewing threads to match fabrics
- Sewing machine

4 Fold the decorative fabric over to lie right side up on the batting, rolling the top edge to the back by a tiny amount so that none of the sturdy fabric shows on the right side. Press the seam flat. Trim off any excess batting and sturdy fabric around the bottom edge. Repeat steps 2 and 3 with the remaining rounded squares.

5 Right side in, fold the loop strip in half lengthwise. Taking a ³⁄₈-in (1-cm) seam allowance, sew the long edge. Turn the tube right side out (see page 128). With the seam along one edge, press the tube flat.

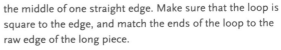

6 Fold the loop strip in half and baste (tack) it to one of the long pieces, in the middle of one straight edge. Make sure that the loop is square to the edge, and match the ends of the loop to the raw edge of the long piece.

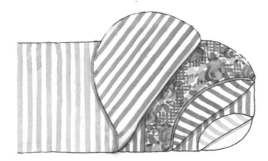

7 Lay the long piece of batting flat. Lay one of the long pieces of sturdy fabric right side up on top of the batting. Then position one mitt section, decorative fabric right side up, at each end of the long piece of fabric. Finally, lay the other long piece of fabric right side down on top of the whole lot. Pin all the layers together.

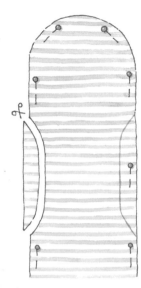

8 At this stage, you can if you want (and I did) shape the strap of the oven glove between the two mitts. I made mine thinner in the middle, just so that it was a little more elegant. Draw shaping onto the fabric using a fabric marker, remembering to include a ⅜-in (1-cm) seam allowance, then cut it out. If you do this, remember to reposition the loop before cutting out the shaping.

9 Sew right around the oven glove, leaving a 4½-in (12-cm) gap in one long edge. Trim the batting back as in Step 3. Turn the glove right side out through the gap and then ladder stitch the gap closed (see page 131). Press the glove flat.

Hot pot MITT

• • • • • • • • • • • • • • • • • • • •

For grabbing warm dishes to take to the table, pulling pie pans out of the oven, picking up a saucepan with a too-warm handle, this practical pot holder is what you need. Use heat-resistant batting (wadding), not the normal quilting stuff—to avoid scorching your fingers—and washable fabrics for practicality.

YOU'RE GOING TO NEED...

- Template on page 136
- Two pieces of outer fabric, two pieces of lining, and two pieces of heat-resistant batting (wadding) each measuring 7 x 9in (18 x 23cm): I used the same cotton for the outer and lining
- One piece of insert fabric, one piece of lining, and one piece of heat-resistant batting each measuring 7 x 10in (18 x 25cm): I used cotton for the lining and corduroy for the insert
- One piece of outer fabric measuring 2 x 7in (5 x 18cm) for the loop, and one piece measuring 2 x 12in (5 x 30cm) for the binding
- Paper for template
- Paper scissors and fabric scissors
- Iron and ironing board
- Pins
- Sewing threads to match fabrics
- Sewing machine

1 Enlarge the template on page 136 by 200 percent. Cut out two outer pieces each from fabric, lining, and batting (wadding). Then cut off the template at the dotted line for the insert piece. Press the insert fabric in half and place the dotted line of the template on the fold, then cut out one insert, cutting through both layers of fabric. Cut an insert from lining and batting in the same way.

2 Right side in, fold the loop strip in half lengthwise. Taking a 3/8-in (1-cm) seam allowance, sew along the long edge. Turn the tube right side out (see page 128). With the seam along one edge, press the tube flat.

3 Fold the loop strip in half and baste (tack) it to one of the outer pieces, 1 1/4in (3cm) up from the straight bottom edge. Make sure that the loop is square to the edge of the outer (basting along the length, as well as across the end, will help with this), and match the ends of the loop to the raw edge of the outer piece.

4 Pin the two outer pieces right sides together. Starting at the straight bottom edge, and taking a 3/8-in (1-cm) seam allowance, sew up 5 1/4 in (13.5cm) of each side, reversing at the end to secure the stitches. On the side with the loop, reverse then sew across the loop ends again for strength.

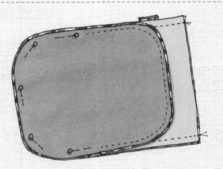

5 Fold back the top outer piece to lie flat, then, right sides together, lay the insert piece on top of the open ends of the outer pieces, matching the raw edges. Pin the insert in place, putting the pins in from the insert side. Starting at the fold of the insert, and taking a 3/8-in (1-cm) seam allowance, sew around one curve of the insert, reversing at both ends to secure the stitches. Repeat the process to sew the other half of the insert in place.

6 Zigzag the seam allowances and trim them, then cut notches (see page 128) in the allowances around the curves. Turn the mitt right side out and press all the seams flat.

7 Baste the batting pieces to the wrong side of the lining pieces (for both the outer and insert pieces), then treat each piece as one layer from now on. Make up the lining as in steps 4–6, but taking 5/8-in (1.5-cm) seam allowances and omitting the loop. Take the basting stitches out and leave this piece inside out. Slide it into the outer mitt.

8 Right side out, press the binding strip in half lengthwise. Open it out flat and press one raw edge in to almost touch the middle fold. Press the other raw edge in to lay 1/8 in (2–3mm) from the middle. Then press the first line again; you've made straight-grain binding with one side wider than the other.

9 Unfold the binding and press under ³⁄₈in (1cm) on one short end. Pin the narrower side of the binding around the bottom of the mitt, right sides together and matching the raw edges. When you get back to the start, overlap the raw end over the folded end by ⅝in (1.5cm) and cut off any excess.

10 Sew the binding to the mitt along the fold line nearest the raw edge.

11 Fold the binding over the raw edge of the mitt to the back; the folded edge should just overlap the line of stitching made in Step 10. On the right side, stitch in the ditch—that is, sew along the seam line between the binding and the fabric—to complete the binding: the stitching should just catch the free folded edge of the binding on the inside.

ROUND AND *round*

• •

When lolling on the couch on a rainy day contemplating one's navel, reading a good book, watching a superbly brainless blockbuster movie, one thing you can't have too many of are pillows. A range of shapes is vital for propping up limbs, books, heads... And different degrees of firmness are useful, too. This pillow is small and soft, as well as good-looking and easy to make.

YOU'RE GOING TO NEED...

- Template on page 140
- Eight pieces of fabric measuring 10⅝ x 6¼in (27 x 16cm), one piece measuring 14½in (37cm) square, and one scrap for covering the button: I used cotton fabrics
- Polyester toy filling
- Small two-hole button
- Paper for template
- Paper scissors and fabric scissors
- Tape measure
- Fabric marker or chalk
- Ruler
- Iron and ironing board
- Pins
- Sewing threads to match fabrics
- Sewing machine
- Hand-sewing needle
- Compasses
- 1½in (4cm) self-cover button kit
- Doll needle
- Strong thread

1 Enlarge the template on page 140 by 200 percent. Cut out eight pieces of fabric. On the wrong side of the pieces, mark sewing lines ⅜in (1cm) in from the edges, as shown. If you can machine sew brilliantly, you don't have to do this, but it doesn't take long and it does help make the piecing quick, easy, and accurate.

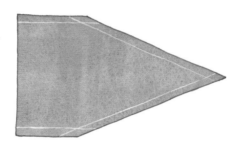

2 Place two pieces right sides together and sew them from the point down to the straight lower edge on one side, reversing at each end to secure the stitching.

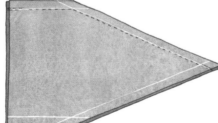

3 Open out the pieces and sew the next piece to the unsewn edge in the same way as Step 2. Continue to sew all the pieces together to make the circular pillow top.

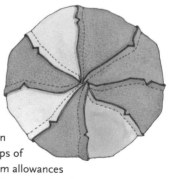

4 Clip a notch (see page 128) into the seam allowances at the curve in each seam. Cut off the tips of the points. Press the seam allowances to one side, all facing in the same direction.

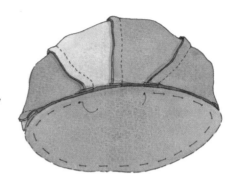

5 Using compasses (or an appropriately sized plate), draw a circle 14in (35cm) in diameter on the large piece of fabric. Cut the circle out. Right sides together, pin then baste (tack) the circle to the raw edge of the pillow top. Taking a 3/8-in (1-cm) seam allowance, sew the seam, leaving a 2-in (5-cm) gap.

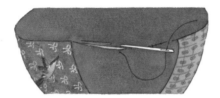

6 Turn the pillow right side out through the gap and press the seam, pressing under the seam allowances across the gap. Fill the pillow with stuffing, then ladder stitch (see page 131) the gap closed.

7 Following the instructions with the button kit, cover the button with fabric. Thread the doll needle with a long length of strong thread, double it, and knot the ends. Make a tiny stitch in the center of the back of the pillow and thread on the small button. Push the needle straight up through the pillow to emerge in the middle of the pillow top (where the points all meet). Thread on the covered button and take the needle back down to emerge through a hole in the small button. Pull the thread taut to indent the buttons into the pillow. Take the needle through the other hole in the small button, but not through the pillow, and secure the thread by looping and knotting it behind the button.

$\mathscr{Bone}$ FIDOS

• • • • • • • • • • • • • • • • • • •

Little Elton likes nothing more than an afternoon of lolling on something soft and cozy. He has beds in various rooms in the house, and staggers from one to another following the sunshine through the day (though as this is England, that often means that he doesn't bother moving much). I made this bed to go in my workroom: it seemed only reasonable that a room used for sewing should have a specially sewn dog bed... There is a bit of optional free-machine embroidery on this project: if you've never tried this technique before, this is a simple starting point.

1 There is a template on page 141 for the bone shape, but rather than trying to enlarge it on lots of bits of paper taped together to make a pattern piece the right size, I suggest you use it as a guide and draw the shape out freehand: it's not a difficult one to draw. On the wrong side of the top piece of fabric, draw the outline and the spirals with the fabric marker.

2 Set your sewing machine for free-machine embroidery (this involves dropping the feed dogs: the manual will tell you how if you've not done it before) and thread it with sewing or machine embroidery thread that will show up well on the fabric. I also use a machine-embroidery needle, as I find that otherwise the thread tends to break if I sew fast. On the wrong side, sew around the spirals using a single line of stitching. Because the embroidered spirals touch the edges of the bone shape, I found it best to do all the embroidery before cutting out the shape.

3 Turn the fabric over and, following the guide line of stitches, embroider the spirals, "scribbling" back and forth with stitches to make a bold line. I didn't use an embroidery hoop, and the fabric did pucker up a bit as the stitching pulled it in, but the furriness is very forgiving and once the bed was stuffed, the puckering smoothed out. Cut out the top piece around the outline and use that as a template to cut out the bottom piece.

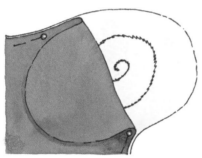

4 Pin the top and bottom right sides together. Taking a 3/8-in (1-cm) seam allowance, sew around the edge, leaving a 4-in (10-cm) gap in the straight middle part of one side. Zigzag or serge (overlock) the edges to neaten them, remembering not to sew across the gap. Turn the bed right side out.

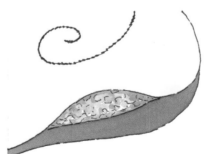

5 Fill the bed with washable stuffing: be aware that this always takes more stuffing than you think it will. Ladder stitch (see page 131) the gap closed. Give your beloved doglet its new bed.

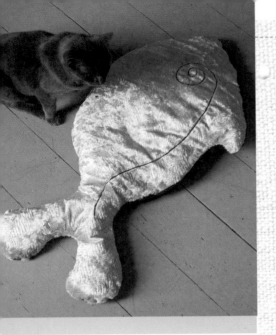

Catfish

Annie is a fickle creature when it comes to favorite places to sleep. For a couple of weeks she'll choose one particular spot, then she'll move on to another, and look at you with astonished disdain if you try to persuade her back to the previous spot: exactly how stupid are you to think that she might want to sleep there? However, this soft, velvety bed has kept her attention for a while now...

YOU'RE GOING TO NEED...

- Template on page 141 (optional)
- Top and bottom fabrics: I used fur fabric for the top and fleece for the bottom; both fabrics are washable. See How Much Fabric?, below
- Paper for templates
- Paper scissors and fabric scissors
- Tape measure
- Fading fabric marker
- Iron and ironing board
- Pins
- Sewing threads to match fabrics
- Sewing machine, preferably with a machine-embroidery needle
- Hand-sewing needle

HOW MUCH FABRIC?

- This depends entirely on how big you want the bed to be. I cut this bed from fabric measuring 33½ x 19in (85 x 48cm).

1 There is a template for the fish shape on page 141, but rather than trying to enlarge it on lots of bits of paper taped together to make a pattern piece the right size, I suggest you use it as a guide and draw the shape out freehand: it's not a difficult one to draw. Cut out the top piece, then use that as a template to cut out the bottom piece.

2 On the wrong side of the top piece, draw the spiral eye with the fabric marker. Set your sewing machine for free-machine embroidery (this involves dropping the feed dogs: the manual will tell you how if you've not done it before) and thread it with sewing or machine embroidery thread that will show up well on the fabric. I also use a machine-embroidery needle, as I find that otherwise the thread tends to break if I sew fast. On the wrong side, sew the spiral and line using a single line of stitching.

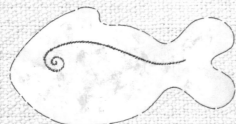

3 Turn the fabric over and, following the guide line of stitches, embroider the spirals, "scribbling" back and forth with stitches to make a bold line. I used an embroidery hoop as the fabric was quite thin and so would have puckered a lot. I just shifted the hoop along as I sewed the line running down to the tail.

4 Pin the top and bottom right sides together. Taking a ³/₈-in (1-cm) seam allowance, sew around the edge, leaving a 4-in (10-cm) gap in the straight middle part of one side. Zigzag or serge (overlock) the edges to neaten them, remembering not to sew across the gap.

5 Fill the bed with washable stuffing, though for maximum fishiness, keep it quite flat rather than stuffing it so full that it becomes rounded. Ladder stitch (see page 131) the gap closed. See if your cat appreciates its new bed…

Techniques

Transferring designs onto fabric

On pages 132–41 are the templates for the projects in this book, and you'll need to transfer them onto fabric if you want to copy a project exactly.

If you only need the outline of a shape, then just enlarge the template to the right size on a photocopier if necessary (all the templates give the correct enlargement percentage), and cut it out. Pin it to the fabric. If you're used to cutting out patterns, or it's a fairly simple shape, just cut out around the edges of the template. Otherwise, draw around it with a fading fabric marker pen (don't be tempted to use an ordinary pen or pencil, as they can permanently mark and spoil your project), then remove the template and cut out the shape.

If there are marks within the template that you need, remember to transfer them onto the fabric, too.

Turning tubes right side out

When making loops or straps, you can use a loop turner to turn the tube right side out. Alternatively, follow this method, using a needle and thread.

1 Thread a blunt-tipped needle (such as a tapestry needle) with a length of strong sewing thread longer than the tube. Knot one end and take it through the seam allowance close to one end of the tube.

2 Gently pull on the needle end of the thread and manipulate the tube with your fingers to turn it right side out. Cut away the thread.

Trimming corners

For corners, you need to snip off the excess fabric across the point before you turn the project right side out, so that the finished corner is neat and square. Cut off the fabric across the corner about ⅛in (2–3mm) away from the stitching, taking care not to cut through the stitches.

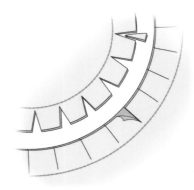

Clipping curved seam allowances

This helps curved seams lie flat and will make a real difference to the look of your finished project.

Use the tips of your fabric scissors (don't use tiny embroidery scissors, as this will dull the blades) to cut into the seam allowance after stitching, taking great care not to cut through any of the stitches. Seams that curve outward need wedge-shaped notches cut into the seam allowance, while for seams that will curve inward, little slits will do (though I usually just cut notches in both types of seam).

Stitches

These are the embroidery and utility hand stitches used in the projects.

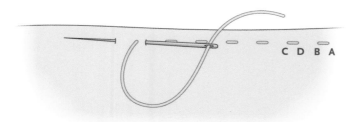

Pick stitch

This is like backstitch, but the stitches on the right side are tiny, and there are gaps between them.

Working from right to left, bring the needle up at A, down at B, and up at C, three stitch lengths ahead of A. Take it down again at D.

Chain stitch

This stitch is easy to work, forgiving of inexperience, and very good-looking.

Bring the needle up at A, then insert it at the same point. Make a short stitch to B, looping the thread under the tip of the needle.

Pull the thread through to form the first loop in the chain. Insert the needle at B again and make another short stitch to C (the same length as the A-to-B stitch), then loop the thread under the tip of the needle. Continue, keeping all the stitches the same length. To anchor the last stitch in the chain, take the needle down just outside the loop, forming a little bar over it.

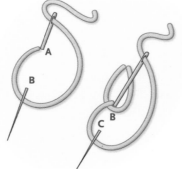
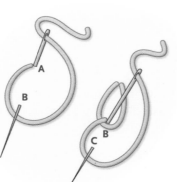

Whip stitch

This is used to join fabrics either right sides or wrong sides together. Hold together the two pieces of fabric, matching the edges to be joined. From the back, take the needle through both pieces, close to the edge. Take the needle over the edges and to the back and through both pieces again a short distance further along, pulling the thread taut to complete the stitch. If you are joining the fabrics wrong sides together, you can hide the starting knot between the layers.

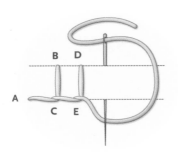
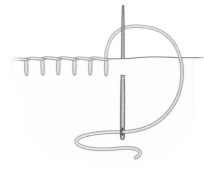
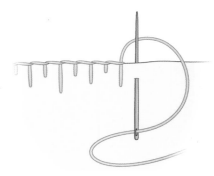

Blanket stitch

Another stitch that's both utility and decorative. Use it to sew one piece of fabric to another, or just as an embroidery stitch, or work it along an edge, or use it to join two edges.

Bring the needle up at A, down at B, and up at C (directly below B), looping the thread under the tip of the needle. Pull the needle through, then insert it at D and bring it out at E, again looping the thread under the tip.

If you are working it along an edge, the principle is the same, but the horizontal bar of thread lies along the edge of the fabric, as shown.

Variation: Irregular blanket stitch

Follow the same method as ordinary blanket stitch, but make each "leg" of the stitch irregular in length.

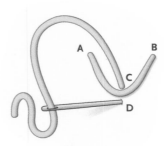

Fly stitch

As well as being great for stitching down buttons decoratively (see page 76), fly stitch is also a lovely embroidery stitch.

Bring the needle up at A and down at B, leaving a loop of thread. Bring the needle up inside the loop at C and pull the loop taut, then take the needle down at D, outside the loop. The C-to-D stitch can be long or short, as you prefer.

Cross stitch

This is a very simple embroidery stitch, though I've used it only for sewing on buttons decoratively.

Bring the needle up through one hole in a four-hole button, then take it down through the hole diagonally opposite. Make another slanting stitch through the remaining two empty holes.

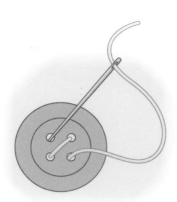

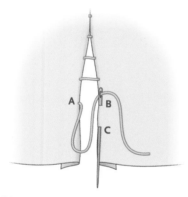

Ladder stitch

This is the best stitch for closing up the gap in a machine- or hand-sewn seam once the project has been turned right side out.

Turn in the seam allowances across the gap and press them (with your fingers or an iron). Bring the needle up through the pressed fold at A, then take it straight across the gap to B. Make a tiny stitch through the folded edge and bring it back to the front at C. Continue in this way, zigzagging from one side to another and making the stitches equally spaced.

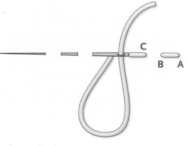

Running stitch

Another multi-purpose stitch: use it for basting (not worrying about stitch length or tidiness), for decoration, or for gathering.

Bring the needle up at A, down at B, and up at C, and continue in this way. If being used decoratively, you can space the stitches evenly and make them all the same length, or work them more randomly, depending on the look you want.

Templates

This section contains all the templates you will need. Where a template is not given at actual size, simply photocopy it at the percentage indicated in order to enlarge it.

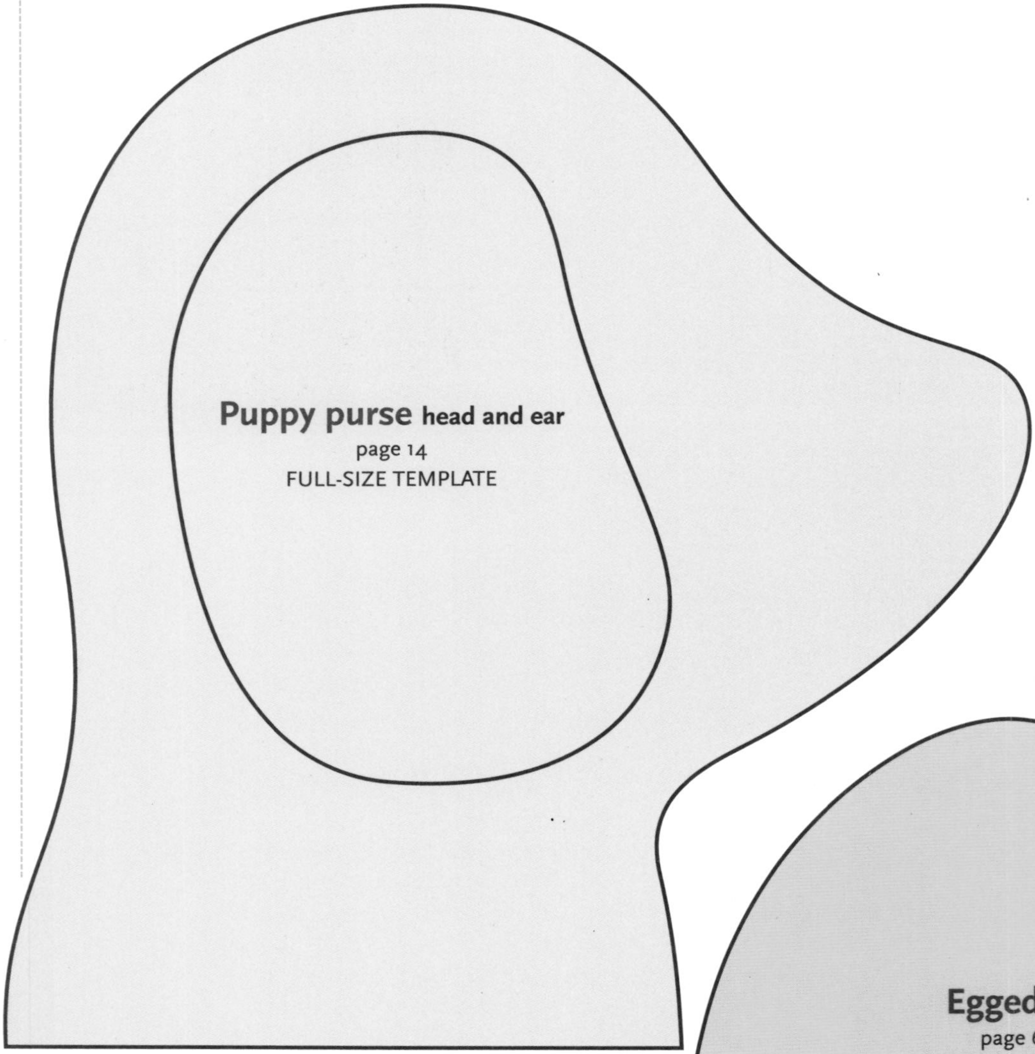

Puppy purse head and ear
page 14
FULL-SIZE TEMPLATE

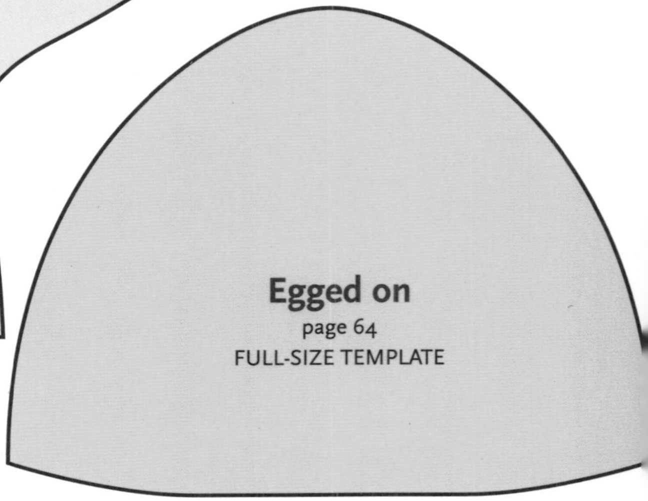

Egged on
page 64
FULL-SIZE TEMPLATE

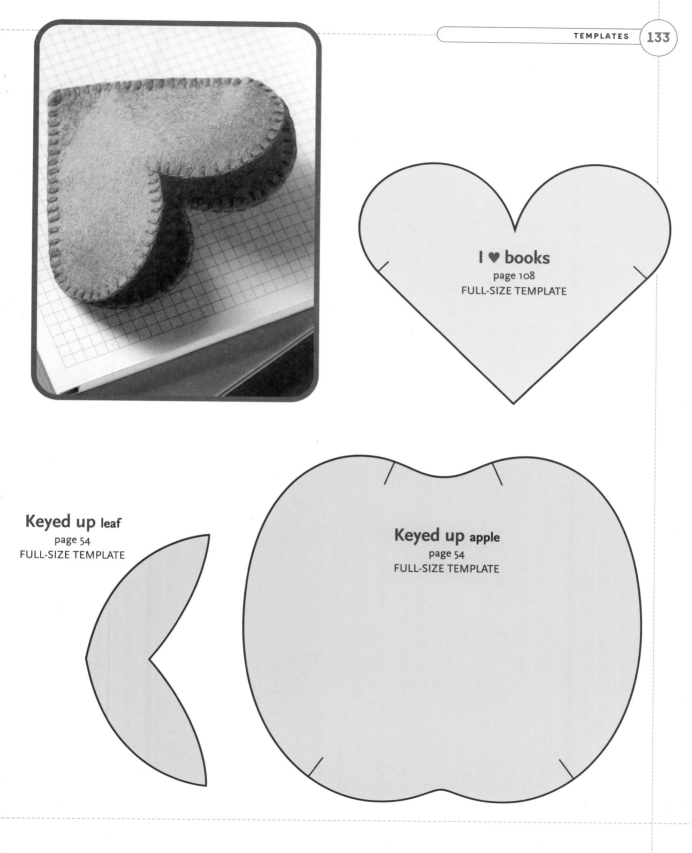

I ♥ books
page 108
FULL-SIZE TEMPLATE

Keyed up leaf
page 54
FULL-SIZE TEMPLATE

Keyed up apple
page 54
FULL-SIZE TEMPLATE

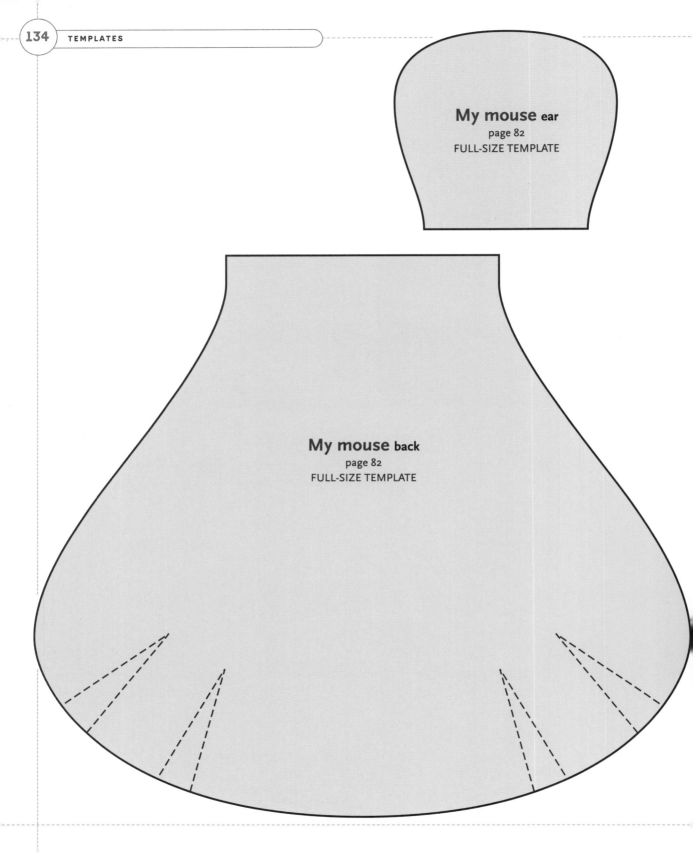

My mouse ear
page 82
FULL-SIZE TEMPLATE

My mouse back
page 82
FULL-SIZE TEMPLATE

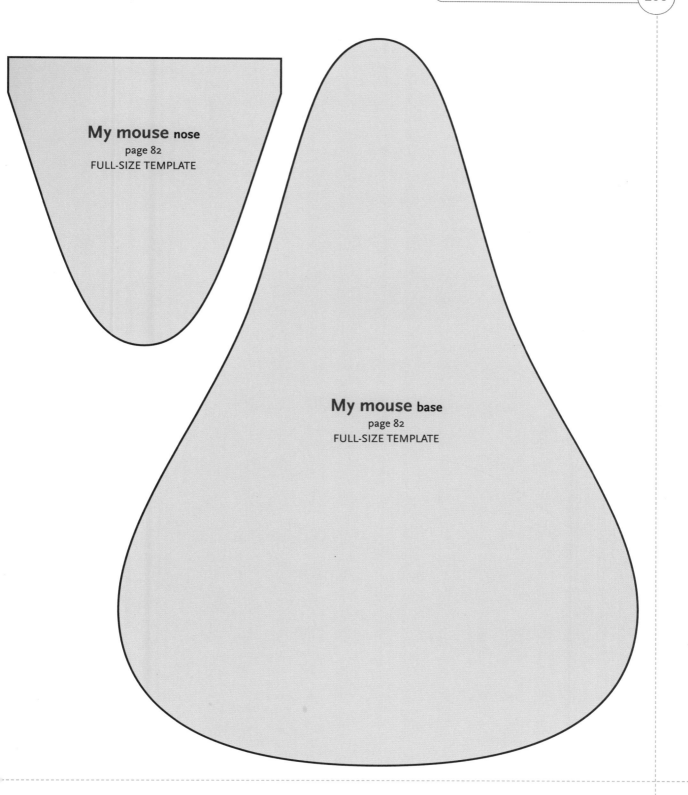

My mouse nose
page 82
FULL-SIZE TEMPLATE

My mouse base
page 82
FULL-SIZE TEMPLATE

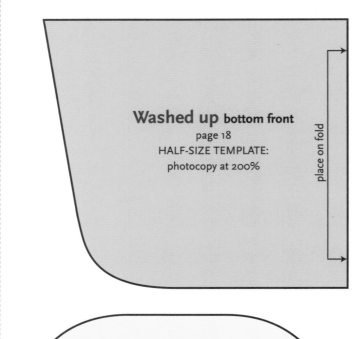

Washed up bottom front
page 18
HALF-SIZE TEMPLATE:
photocopy at 200%

place on fold

Washed up top front
page 18
HALF-SIZE TEMPLATE:
photocopy at 200%

place on fold

Hot pot mitt
page 116
HALF-SIZE TEMPLATE:
photocopy at 200%

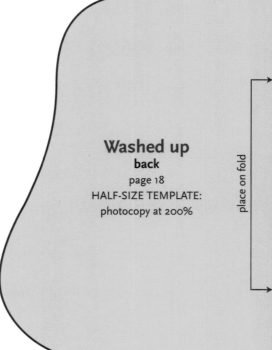

Washed up
back
page 18
HALF-SIZE TEMPLATE:
photocopy at 200%

place on fold

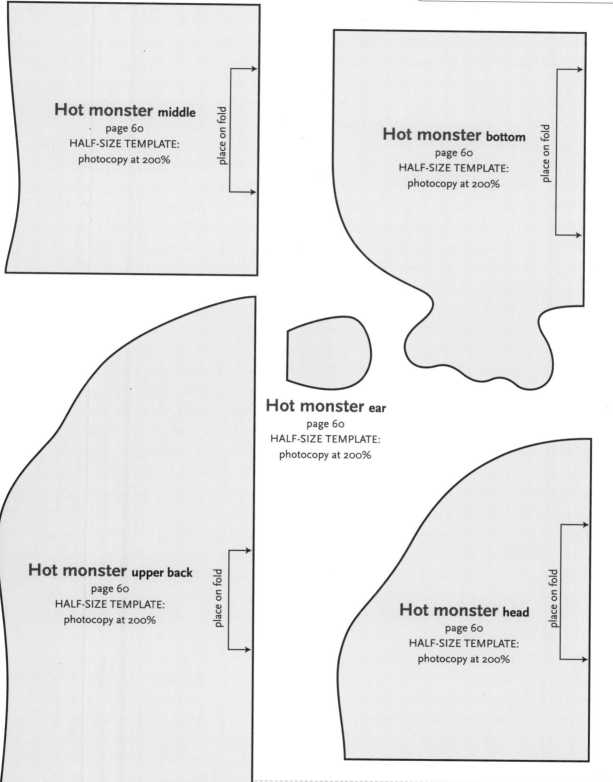

Hot monster middle
page 60
HALF-SIZE TEMPLATE:
photocopy at 200%

place on fold

Hot monster bottom
page 60
HALF-SIZE TEMPLATE:
photocopy at 200%

place on fold

Hot monster ear
page 60
HALF-SIZE TEMPLATE:
photocopy at 200%

Hot monster upper back
page 60
HALF-SIZE TEMPLATE:
photocopy at 200%

place on fold

Hot monster head
page 60
HALF-SIZE TEMPLATE:
photocopy at 200%

place on fold

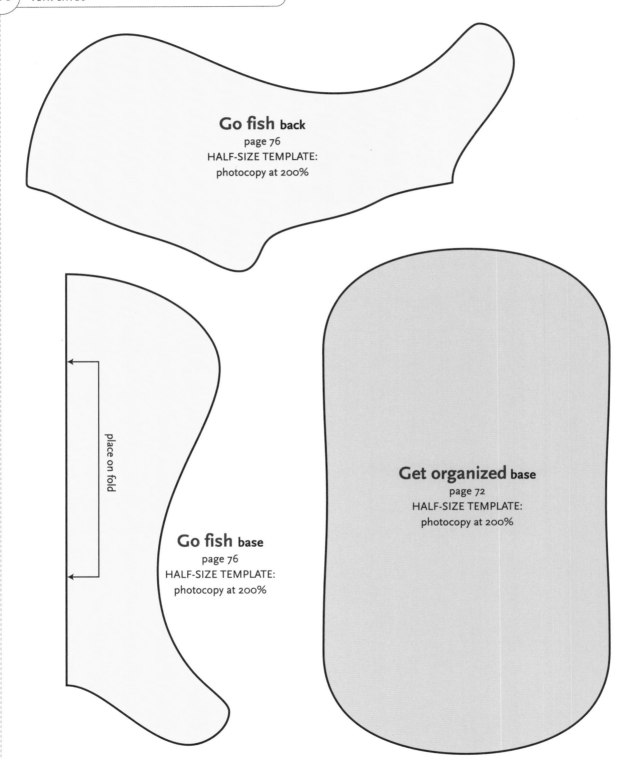

Go fish back
page 76
HALF-SIZE TEMPLATE:
photocopy at 200%

place on fold

Go fish base
page 76
HALF-SIZE TEMPLATE:
photocopy at 200%

Get organized base
page 72
HALF-SIZE TEMPLATE:
photocopy at 200%

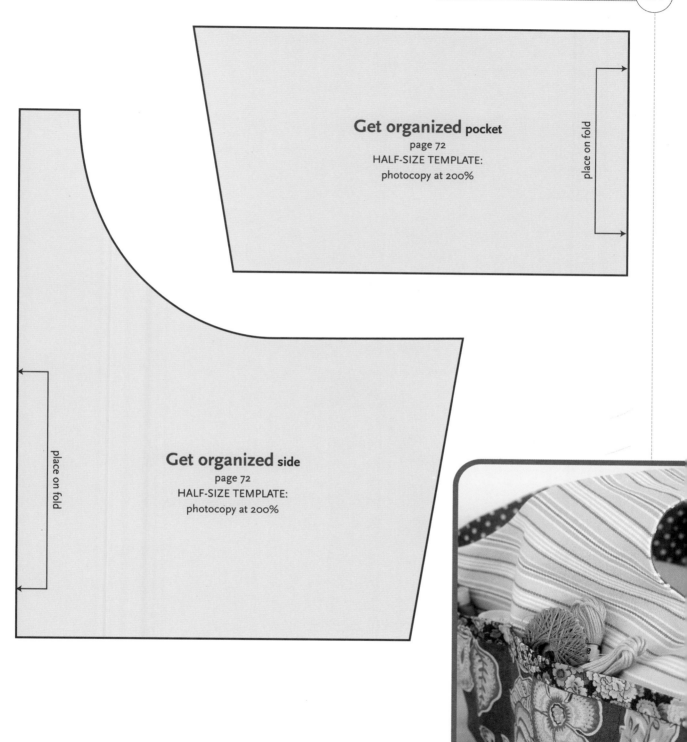

Get organized pocket
page 72
HALF-SIZE TEMPLATE:
photocopy at 200%

place on fold

Get organized side
page 72
HALF-SIZE TEMPLATE:
photocopy at 200%

place on fold

Round and round
page 120
HALF-SIZE TEMPLATE:
photocopy at 200%

Tied up
page 38
QUARTER-SIZE
TEMPLATE:
photocopy at 400%

place on fold

DIAGRAMS

These are diagrams to use as a guide—copy them at whatever
size you require for your pet.

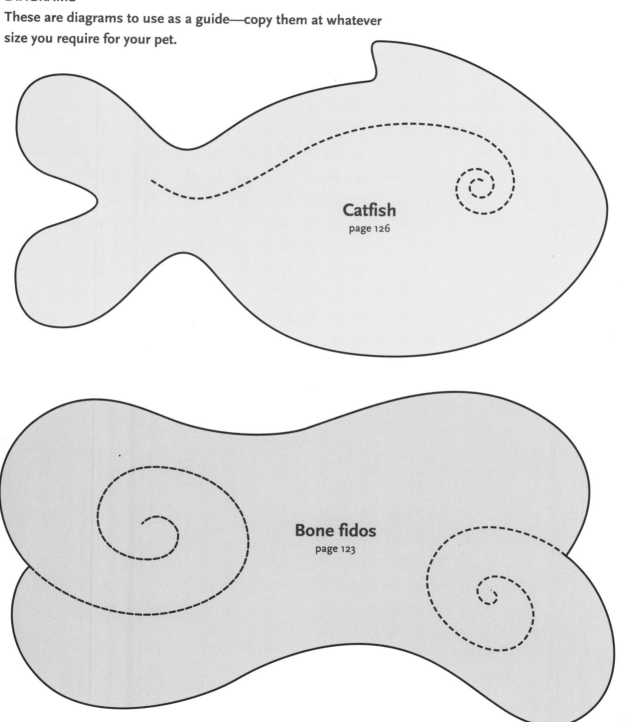

Catfish
page 126

Bone fidos
page 123

Suppliers

US stores

Fabricland
www.fabricland.com

J&O Fabrics
www.jandofabrics.com

Jo-Ann Fabric and Craft Stores
www.joann.com

Michaels Stores
www.michaels.com

Hobby Lobby
www.hobbylobby.com

Purl Soho
www.purlsoho.com

UK stores

John Lewis
www.johnlewis.com
Great sewing equipment and some fabrics.

Liberty
www.liberty.co.uk
Lovely sewing equipment, notions (haberdashery), and fabrics.

Fabrics Galore
www.fabricsgalore.co.uk
Always my first stop on a fabric shop. Great range at excellent prices.

Creative Quilting
www.creativequilting.co.uk
Good range of fabrics and very helpful staff. They also sell some embroidery floss (thread) and sewing equipment.

The Cloth House
www.clothhouse.com
My favorite fabric shop, with a range of acrylic/wool mix felts.

Guthrie & Ghani
www.guthrie-ghani.co.uk
Lovely fabrics and notions, and lovely staff.

Index

. . . .

Acknowledgments

My thanks to Cindy Richards at CICO for suggesting this addition to the *Sewlicious* family, and to Carmel Edmonds for keeping it all on track. My thanks to Katie Hardwicke for all her hard work at the editorial coalface; to Jo Henderson, Sania Pell, and Luis Peral for the gorgeous photos; to Carrie Hill for the good-looking and informative illustrations; and to Elizabeth Healey for putting it all together so beautifully. As ever, I have Philip to thank for feeding me.